The Streets Of LaGrange

Jimmy McPhail

ISBN: 978-1-961677-34-0 (Paperback)

Library of Congress Control Number: 2023915584

Printed in the United States of America

Published by:

info@thequippyquill.com
(302) 295-2278

This book is dedicated to the oppressed, downtrodden, and reputable people of LaGrange. May your stories live on

Contents

Acknowledgments

Ralph Waldo Emerson once said, "Vigor is contagious, and whatever makes us either think or feel strongly adds to our power and enlarges our field of action." During the days, weeks, months and years that it took me to gather information and pen the words that are found within the context of this book, there were a lot of people who worked vigorously to help me realize this goal.

Among them were:

My wife Cheryl, who held my hand, ran numerous errands and deposited within me words of encouragement when I needed them the most.

My brother Charles, who provided pertinent information about the police department, as well as allowing me to share his personal story.

My children, Desmond and Brittany. Thank you for helping me gather information, making phone calls, running errands...and everything else you've done to support me in this endeavor.

The residents of LaGrange. Thank you for granting me permission to share your stories.

And finally, writer J. B. Morrisey, through whose talents this book was edited and written.

It is because of these people that I think and feel strongly about this book and my field of action is enlarged.

-Jimmy McPhail

Preface

"Get off my sidewalk, you little niggers." Those were the words she yelled as she tossed rocks from her yard and whatever other objects she could find to help get her point across. The year was 1974 and summer vacation had just begun. My brother, sister, and a couple of our cousins were walking down the sidewalk along West Railroad Street in LaGrange, North Carolina when the incident occurred.

The kids, ranging in age, from six to eleven, were shocked at first, but then dismissed the occurrence, thinking that the elderly lady must have been slightly "off her rocker." But, after retelling the incident to other people in the community, people who were familiar with the lady's values and beliefs in regards to people of color, my family and I realized that the old lady wasn't crazy at all. She meant what she said, and she said what she meant. She had very little tolerance for African Americans, looking down upon them and viewing them as less human than she or any of her white counterparts.

My family had moved to the town of LaGrange a few months prior to the incident on West Railroad Street. Up until then, we had lived deep in the country, where tobacco farming and grooming livestock were at the core of my summer enrichment program. Mama and Daddy both had jobs in Kinston. Daddy worked at Smithfields, a processing plant for hams. His brother, Lawyer, lived in Snow Hill, and was most likely the reason that my father and mother decided to relocate to the area.

Mama worked for a female doctor at her house. I don't remember the doctor's name, or even the type of medicine that he practiced. What I remember most about Mama's work was that it was hard and extremely taxing on her body. I was glad when she was finally able to move on to something better.

My siblings and I (fourteen of us, altogether) spent a great deal of our time working in corn, tobacco and cucumber fields. We had never been privy to the many conveniences and niceties that were afforded to people living within city limits. So, for us, the move into town was almost like a dream come true.

The post office. grocery store, corner market, and even the school were within walking distance. When we lived in the country, we were fortunate, at best, to be able to go into town only once or twice a week. But having a permanent dwelling in town meant that we could visit the corner market once or twice a day. Providing we had money, of course!

For the most part, my childhood and adolescent years were quite wholesome. Our fourteen-member household was big in number, but also big in love. Mama and Daddy both worked hard and expected none less from their hearty offspring. So, when the time came for me to leave the family nest and venture out on my own, I felt confident in my in-bred skills, experiences, and abilities. Like my parents, I, too, was compelled to make my family's abode in LaGrange. At that time (the early '80s), the population was about 2.600, with African Americans comprising about half of that figure. Most of the people were hard working, blue-collar individuals. There was very little crime, noise, or disturbances of any kind. I just knew that I would be living out the American dream.

But as the weeks, months, and years passed by, my dream of living in LaGrange began to grow into an unpleasant nightmare; a nightmare that has been tainted with the ugly stains or racism, discrimination and hatred that has become an all too familiar way of life for African American residents. Justice and equality are foreigners that visit our city during election time, but pack up their bags and move on, very shortly, thereafter. Stories of racism, harassment, police brutality and, the like, are commonplace occurrences for LaGrange residents...or at least those residents of color.

But don't take my word for it. In the pages that follow, you'll be able to meet some of the local residents, hear their stories, experience their shame, and share their pain. You'll soon learn that hearing someone tell you to "get off my sidewalk," or having someone call you a "nigger" is really not the worst thing that could happen to a person of color. Believe me, it gets worse.

We must remember that....
any oppression
any injustice
any hatred
is a wedge
designed to attack our civilization.

-Franklin D. Roosevelt

The Resolution

Anger and Disbelief. Those were the first two emotions that I can remember feeling when council members began their discussion of the proposed resolution. It was Item 6E on the agenda.

It was February 3, 1997, and I was one of many in attendance that night at the regular session meeting of the town council of LaGrange. We were about halfway into the meeting by then and, with the exception of the mayor's report on the negative feedback that he had received from last month's meeting. things seemed to be progressing along rather well.

When the council began their discussion of Item 5: Amendments to the Agenda, Mayor Keaton opened up the topic with his most recent disclosure. According to the mayor, many questions had been asked of him concerning my request to appear before the town council in the January 6th meeting. Most of the questions had centered around his actions or, maybe, the lack, thereof, to silence me from voicing my concerns and the legitimate concerns of others about Chief Sutton and his use of discriminatory tactics that had become common practice throughout the police department. Once given the floor to speak, I didn't waste time mixing words. I went straight to the heart of the matter. For years, I had sat and idly watched as problems surmounted and hostility intensified between black citizens and members of the police department. Most of my accusations were directed at Chief Sutton, who, in my opinion, was at the root of the problem. In my personal experiences with him, Chief Sutton had falsified a report to place my son at fault for an accident in which he was faultless, and had been instrumental in getting my brother relieved from his duties as Assistant Chief of Police. And while these were legitimate issues of personal concern, I knew of more than twenty other black citizens who had been on the receiving end of Chief Sutton's unfair practices and/or the unscrupulous law enforcement practices of his officers. I warned the council of the need for them to intervene before a major tragedy occurred in our city. The way I saw it, Chief Sutton was a walking time bomb. Chief Sutton was operating the police department under racially-based initiatives and those practices needed to come to an end.

Apparently, a select few of the citizens in attendance the previous month had questioned whether or not such an attack on a leader's competence and character should be permissible in a public forum and whether or not harsh language could be used. The mayor made it perfectly clear to everyone that he was not afraid to raise the gavel, but at the time did not feel the need to do so. The way Mayor Keaton saw it, every single word that I had spoken that night could be found in the dictionary, and as long as the words were not taken out of context, they were, indeed, allowable in a public meeting. And if that wasn't enough to satisfy the pretentious council and the wayward townspeople, Mayor Keaton formally apologized in the event that he had committed a wrongdoing in not raising the gavel.

At that point, I have to admit, my mind began to wander. I allowed my eyes the freedom and flexibility to scan the room. With my mind intrigued, I tried to mentally decipher the individuals who would have most likely questioned the mayor's actions. A few of Chief Sutton's cronies jumped to the forefront of my mental image. It was easy to figure out where the councilmen stood. Their views were evident in the statements that they made, both during meetings and within the community. But some of the other faces seemed less predictable. Those that perplexed me the most were the people who engaged themselves in shallow conversations about work, family and the like, but straddled the fence when it came to heavy duty topics, such as politics, religion, or any subject that would require them to take a stand and speak their conviction. Mayor Keaton was a stand taker, and for that reason, alone, he was highly favored in my book. I didn't appreciate the grief that he had received in not raising the gavel, but I applauded him in his ability to take a stand for what was right, even if that meant standing alone. Mayor Keaton was a highly respected individual, known throughout the community. During his reign as mayor, he had played an active role in ensuring fair and equal treatment of all residents and in helping the town establish an atmosphere of unity and cohesiveness. None of the other mayors had ever been able to do that, and I seriously doubted whether or not anyone else ever could.

After the mayor had ended his dialogue concerning the complaints that had arisen during the January 6th meeting, he moved the council members on with the agenda in his usual format. The next half hour or so of the meeting seemed somewhat dry with discussions of such topics as the downtown revitalization project and recommendations from the planning and zoning board. I really wasn't concerned with either of the two topics, and the council must have voted to table those issues because there was very little discussion and neither matter was put to vote.

But when the council began their discussion of Item 6E: Resolution of Support to Chief of Police, I think that the hairs on the back of my neck surely must have stood at attention. Councilman Washington, a man who had pledged his undying support to Chief Sutton on numerous occasions, introduced the resolution to the council. As Lloyd explained, the resolution was in response to the attack that was made (by me) on Chief Sutton's character in the January meeting. By signing the resolution, the mayor and all of the members of the council would be able to publicly display their unified support of the police chief. The resolution read as follows:

Whereas, John L. Sutton Jr., serves as the Chief of Police for the Town of LaGrange; and
Whereas, he has demonstrated his deep and genuine concern for the Town of LaGrange; and
Whereas, Town Council supports his performance of the duties and responsibilities as Chief of Police for the Town of LaGrange; and
Whereas, Town Council will continue to support him to carry out the duties and responsibilities of that position in accordance with local, state and federal regulations and requirements.

Now, THEREFORE BE IT RESOLVED THAT THE Town fr of LaGrange, and on behalf of all our citizens, adopt this resolution on the 3rd day of February, 1997.

The resolution passed with a 4-2 vote and with no further ado, the council proceeded with the remaining items on the agenda and I stood there for a while, shaking my head in utter disbelief. Not only had the council failed to put an end to Chief Sutton's callous acts of bigotry, but in all practical ways, they had pinned him with a badge of honor and given him a four man salute.

In hindsight, I guess the signing of the resolution wasn't all bad. It helped open the eyes of many black and white residents and encouraged them to start thinking about the way the city was being run. My eye opening experience had occurred nearly twenty years prior to the February 3rd town meeting, around the time of Lonnie George's death. Before that time, I suppose that I must have made up excuses to explain the tiny little idiosyncrasies of the legal and judicial system that slightly differed when it came to black and white relations. Either that, or I must have learned to look the other way, thinking that the less trouble you stir up, the less there'll be. Like the time Walter Chestnutt went to town hall to pay his utility bill and complained about how high it was. He was told that if he kept complaining, his bill would never go down. Walter didn't want any trouble, so he stopped complaining.

But after reading the rose-colored writeup in the Weekly Gazette that chronicled the events leading up to George's death, I found it literally impossible to keep quiet or to look the other way. According to the paper, on the evening of April 26, 1981, Mr. Lonnie George was found standing at the edge of his residence wearing a pair of socks as his only remnant of clothing. After a few of the local residents witnessed Mr. George's obscenity, the LaGrange Police Department was notified and Assistant Chief Charles Bosworth was the first to respond to the call. Because George's residence was located outside the city limits, Basden contacted the Lenoir County Sheriff's Department for backup. Deputy Sheriff Paul Edwards answered the call.

After perceiving the intent of the law enforcement officers to take him into custody, Mr. George attempted to find refuge inside his residence. Chief Basden followed the seventy-two-year-old black male into his mobile home, spraying him with mace and forcing him to exit the premises. When George emerged, he brought with him an iron pipe, which the police "suspected" would be used against them.

Basden and Casey concocted a plan that entailed Casey circling around the rear of the residence and apprehending George from behind. However, before the plan could be fully executed, George, reportedly, became extremely violent and aggressive, backing Basden up to a wall. Basden grabbed his gun and fired a warning shot, but the scare tactic did not seem to faze George. When Basden realized that George was not intimidated by his position of authority, he pointed his .38 caliber gun directly at George's chest and fired.

The LaGrange Rescue Squad was notified and George was rushed to Lenoir Memorial Hospital. However, despite their prompt arrival and life- saving efforts rendered, George was declared dead on arrival.

After the shooting incident occurred, some of the local residents began to speculate about the actual progression of events that had taken place. Had Mr. George's capture been handled differently, wouldn't he be alive today? Were not Assistant Chief Basden and Deputy Sheriff Casey aware of Mr. George's history of mental illness?

Following the incident, an investigation by the State Bureau of Investigations ensued. As a routine procedure, Basden was suspended, indefinitely, with pay. Black citizens became enraged and organized a march, while several white citizens sold barbecue plates in an attempt to offset the cost of Basden's attorney fees.

At the trial, Deputy Sheriff Casey testified that he had been in a position to apprehend Mr. George by grabbing him from behind but was instructed by Basden to step out of the way. "I'm gonna shoot the son of a bitch," jeered Basden. But even with this inflammatory statement, a jury of Basden's "peers" found him innocent of all charges.

The day after the trial ended, I found myself engaged in conversations with others who shared my own personal feelings of defeat. No, I wasn't the victim, nor the assailant in the case, but I felt like a part of me had gone to trial. I wanted so badly for George's death to be avenged and for his murderers to receive some form of punishment. That would have been one sure way to help me dispel my doubts and restore my belief in the American system of equality and justice for all.

But as the trial came to a disheartening end, my faith in LaGrange's police department and judicial system seemed to fizzle. We, as minorities, had lost the battle for democracy once again. The officer who had taken an oath to protect the citizens of LaGrange was given a free pass to commit murder. How could this be? After hearing the slanderous remarks he had made, before and after pulling the trigger, how was it that a jury of his peers could find him innocent of all charges? How could a just police department support his actions?

The more I thought about the outcome of the trial, the more questions began to form in my mind. I couldn't let the questions go. I had to find the answers. Did others share my views about the corrupt system of management or was it just me?

Seven years earlier, I would not have been able to formulate such questions in my mind, especially just being introduced to the convenience of LaGrange's town living. I was too caught up in the excitement and splendor of city life that I missed the message that the racist, rock throwing lady was trying to send. That day when she hurled rocks at my family and ordered us to get off "her" sidewalk, she, like Lonnie George's murderer, knew that there would be no repercussions. She had hated my family without a cause and felt that she could invoke any method of treatment upon us that she deemed appropriate. In 1974, I was a mere teen, made to feel frightened and awkward in the presence of whites. But in 1985, I was a husband and a father. I worked for a successful company and made a comfortable living. I was confident in who I was and how I expected to be treated by others. Being looked upon as a second class citizen was not on my list of expectations.

When I sat out to unmask the subtle forms of inequality that were running rampant in LaGrange's system of town management and local police department, I had no idea what I might find. But I learned, somehow, along the way, that if you ask enough questions, pretty soon you'll start finding answers. For more than twenty years I've been reading the papers and listening to the disturbing stories of others-stories of discrimination, harassment, racial profiling, and the like. I've heard stories of murder, unlawful arrests, police brutality and other stories that if I didn't already know them to be true, would have trouble myself believing. These stories, which were somehow left out of the papers, made a lasting impact on the residents of LaGrange. Whether they were affected physically, spiritually or mentally, the lives of these residents will forever be scarred by the abuse and unfair treatment that they received on the Streets of LaGrange.

Too Many Disturbing Stories

Assistant Chief Gets Shafted

Hard work, perseverance and attention to detail are all noteworthy qualities in the world of work. But in one man's situation, these notable attributes were rewarded with a letter of termination.

With the unfavorable outcome of the Lonnie George murder case, black citizens throughout LaGrange became enraged. The police department, who at the time did not have a single black police officer on their payroll, felt the need to try and make amends. Shortly after George's death the police department ran an ad in the local newspaper with the intent of hiring a black officer in an effort to ease tension within the city.

When my brother Charles saw the ad, he joked with our mother about applying for the position. Charles knew that while he had no prior police experience whatsoever, he was well liked and respected throughout the community. For more than eight years, residents had watched from afar as he volunteered his time with the students at LaGrange Elementary. In the mid '70s and '80s, rural cities such as LaGrange could not afford to fund physical education departments at the elementary school level. Schools such as LaGrange Elementary depended on people like Charles to volunteer their services and help the schools meet the educational needs of its students. The school was more than fortunate to have someone like Charles volunteering his time as a non-paid member of the staff.

Mama, being the optimist that she was, encouraged Charles to apply for the position. "It won't hurt to try," she said. "And who knows? You just might get it."

Well, as luck would have it, Mama was right. In May of 1981, Chief Ronnie Price offered Charles the position and on June 1, he became LaGrange's first black police officer.

In those days, police officers could be hired without any prior law enforcement education or experience. Officers like my brother Charles received on-the-job training in areas of patrolling, investigations, enforcing traffic laws and things of that nature. When a slot became available at the Wilson Police Academy, the officer would be sent there for about seven weeks to receive formal training. Charles was able to receive about six months' worth of on-the-job training before a slot opened up for him in January 1982.

For the next two years, Charles served the police department in the capacity of a patrolman, but completed other duties as well. Taking note of his tenacity and attention to detail, Chief Price promoted Charles to the position of sergeant in 1983. Four years later in 1987, Charles was awarded the title of Assistant Police Chief.

Serving in the capacity of Assistant Chief suited my brother well. He worked well with people and maintained accurate and detailed records. When Chief Price was absent or away from the office, Charles single-handedly ran the department. Aside from a few minor confrontations with disgruntled traffic violators and the tedious amount of paperwork required of his position, Charles enjoyed his job and the work that he did each day as Assistant Police Chief.

In the Spring of 1993, Chief Price announced his plans for retirement. Everyone knew that with Charles being the Assistant Police Chief, he would be the most likely candidate to fill the chief's vacancy: however, becoming chief was not on Charles' list of long range goals. In the thirteen years that he had worked for the police department, Charles had gained a wealth of knowledge about matters pertaining to the legal system. The pecking order for lawsuits was a procedure that he had learned early-on. As Charles explained it, every officer on the police department had a million dollars worth of insurance coverage. If an altercation arose between a citizen and an officer resulting in a lawsuit being filed, the suit would begin with the police chief, the Town, and then the officer. If the suit awarded was in excess of a million dollars, it would be the chief's responsibility to come up with the rest. Having that threat was enough to steer Charles away from applying for the chief's position.

Thinking that Charles would surely apply for the position, town officials began to seek out ways to block his path. One of the commissioners was quoted on several occasions by stating, "before we have a nigger as chief, we'll disband the police department." And that's just what they sought to do.

Shortly after Chief Price's retirement announcement was made public, town officials toyed with the idea of having the sheriff's department cover all of the policing duties of LaGrange. Lenoir County Sheriff Bobby Jones was called in and the idea was proposed to him. Had the sheriff's department agreed to take over LaGrange's law enforcement duties, town officials would have lost their voice in the way police matters were handled. Thus, the plan of disbanding the police department and having an outside source take over was discarded.

While the board's first plan to keep Charles from becoming chief failed, their second one was a huge success. In May, 1993, the board met in closed session and made the decision to strip every police officer of his rank. This meant that whether a person had worked for the department for ten years, or whether he had worked for ten days, he would still be classified as a patrolman. Charles had spent more than twelve years working his way through the ranks, and in a matter of just a couple of hours, the time that it took for the board to reach consensus, he had been demoted to the position that he first held back in 1981. He was outraged to know that the council members would rather entrust the city's police department into the hands of an illiterate white man such as Chief Pelletier rather than a competent black such as himself. Although Pelletier sported the title of Police Chief, Charles had been the one who wrote out all of the reports, created the schedules and carried out the administrative duties of the department.

Outraged and offended by his predicament and that of other members of the police department, Charles contacted the Equal Employment Opportunity Commission and filed a complaint. The commission investigated the matter, and three weeks later issued Charles a letter, giving him the right to file suit. In all, there were about six charges filed, including discrimination and failure to be promoted. In order for the charges to stick, Charles' attorney urged him to apply for the chief's position, otherwise there would be no way to argue that he had been discriminated against or un-rightly passed over for the position. Per the attorney's request, my brother submitted his application.

I'm not sure exactly what happened to his application, but I feel reasonably assured that Charles was never considered for the position. With nearly thirteen years of experience in the police department, more than twenty-five years as an active member of our society, and for all practical purposes the most likely candidate for the position, Charles was not even called in for an interview. Town officials were looking for someone who was white, inside and out. They wanted someone who would support their views and scandalous tactics used in operating the town. In December of 1993, the mayor, town manager, and members of the town board found such a person. Jim Sutton, former chief of the Freemont police department, was offered the position and, as fate would have it, he graciously accepted.

In their first couple of months together, Charles and Chief Sutton seemed to hit it off well. On numerous occasions, Chief Sutton commended my brother on his distinguished work ethics and high-quality performance. In February of the following year, Sutton expressed an interest in rewarding Charles' hard work with a promotion. Sutton shared his thoughts in regards to Charles with. then mayor, Randolph Pridgen during a face-to-face meeting at the LaGrange Fire Station. According to Pridgen in a sworn affidavit dated November 14, 1995, during their discussion, Chief Sutton informed Mayor Pridgen that, "Officer McPhail was doing a good job; that his performance appraisals were satisfactory; and that Chief Sutton was considering Charles McPhail for an upgrade from his position as officer to a higher position." His (Sutton's) intent was to have both a white and a black police captain. My brother Charles would be named the black captain and one of Sutton's buddies, then a full-time milk truck driver, would be the white captain.

But when Sutton caught wind of the pending lawsuit, his opinion in regards to Charles' work performance began to change. In a May 1994, evaluation of Charles' work performance, Sutton had nothing but negative things to say. In nearly every single aspect of the evaluation, Sutton checked the box titled, NEEDS IMPROVEMENT and in one area, UNSATISFACTORY. It is important to note that not once during the preceding twelve years of his tenure with the police department had Charles ever received a performance evaluation that was less than satisfactory. It was apparent that Chief Sutton's ulterior motive was to depict Charles in an unfavorable manner and have him officially terminated from the police department. With one too many negative performance evaluations, the chief's quest would prove to be successful.

After the evaluation, Sutton agreed to re-evaluate Charles in about thirty days to give him an opportunity to improve his work performance. As always, Charles worked hard; maybe a little bit harder than usual; but still to no avail. The second evaluation was just as terrible as the first. By that time Charles had realized what was going on. No matter how hard he worked or how good he did his job, a favorable evaluation would not be received. Without a doubt, Chief Sutton saw the lawsuit as a threat to him and the entire department.

His only hope would be to eradicate my brother from the police department, and that's exactly what he did.

Sutton agreed to give Charles one more opportunity to improve his performance. In approximately thirty days (sometime in late August or early September), he would receive a third evaluation. But, before the month's end, stress and anxiety began to wear Charles down and he was forced to go out on medical leave. Per his doctor's request, Charles was instructed to take his medication and recuperate at home. The doctor wrote a letter to that effect and a copy was forwarded to Chief Sutton. Regardless of the doctor's note, Sutton planned to complete the third evaluation within the agreed upon time frame. He telephoned Charles at home and requested that he come in to complete the evaluation.

Feeling somewhat railroaded, my brother contacted his attorney about the situation. In response, the attorney drafted a letter to this affect:

> My client, Mr. Charles McPhail, is under the care of a doctor and will be following his doctor's instructions. With the medication that he is currently taking, the doctor does not feel that it would be safe for Mr. McPhail to fulfill his duties at the police department. Once released from the doctor's care, Mr. McPhail will return to work and complete his evaluation.

Charles felt confident that the letter from the attorney would be enough to appease Chief Sutton and get him off his back, but in just a few days he found out that his line of thinking was all wrong. In November 1994, while out on sick leave, Charles received a certified letter from Town Manager Mason Wynn indicating that his services were no longer needed with the town of LaGrange.

Death in December

For most people, Christmas is a time of year that is filled with joy, excitement and wonder. But in 1937, one young man's sense of seasonal wonder turned to doom when he was maliciously shot and killed for a crime that he did not commit.

On a cold and gloomy December afternoon in the height of the Christmas season, a young black male by the name of Eddie Moore visited Thomas Toys in search of a special gift for one of his siblings. His mother was shopping at one of the stores across the street and the two planned to meet back up within minutes. Not wanting to keep his mother waiting. Eddie moved at a brisk pace throughout the store.

While browsing the aisles and taking in all of the shiny wonders of the season, his tenacious eyes fell upon a tiny elf-like figurine. Eddie carefully lifted the figurine from its resting place on the shelf and fondled it gingerly in his hands for closer inspection. While that may not have been the item that he selected, Eddie must have anticipated that the perfect gift was somewhere lurking on the shelves of the small nickel and dime store.

As he continued his search down the aisle, Eddie barely noticed the approaching figure. It really wasn't until she shrieked and scowled that Eddie realized what had happened. His body had accidentally brushed up against a middle-aged white female. She gasped at Eddie's gall and walked hurriedly down the aisle to report the incident to the store owner.

In her fear and furry, she stammered to get the words out. "Help me! Call the police. That nigger... (pointing her finger in the direction of where Eddie stood) ...touched...me. You gotta hurry...before he tries to get away. I've been attacked!"

Felix Thomas, the storeowner, made the call at once.

In the meantime, Eddie made his selection and proceeded to the counter for checkout. (The lady had left the store by then.) Not wanting to alert Eddie that the police were on their way, Thomas rang up the item, placed it securely in a brown paper bag and bid Eddie and the members of his family to have a safe and Merry Christmas.

Eddie thanked Thomas kindly and headed out of the store to meet back up with his mom. He was barely beyond the store awning's reach when the shots were fired. The anxious rookie police officer didn't waste time asking questions. He just pointed his gun and fired. Eddie fell to the ground and died. His mother, who had been walking in the direction of Thomas Toys, watched him fall.

Man's Best Friend

When a murder occurs in most American cities, local authorities are dispersed to the scene of the crime and an investigation is begun. When the suspect is caught, he is most likely brought to trial and made to suffer and/or make restitution for the crime that he has committed. But when a furry member of Charles McPhail's family is abducted under false pretense, hid and murdered, vital evidence is disregarded and justice fails to be served.

Sam, a brown and tan German shepherd was the trusted companion of Assistant Police Chief Charles McPhail. According to McPhail, Sam was a well-trained guard dog that possessed a gentle spirit and meant no harm to anyone.

On the evening of March 2, 1989, upon his arrival home, McPhail noticed that Sam was missing. McPhail began to search in the woods behind his house and other areas throughout the neighborhood, but to no avail. Sam was nowhere to be found. His only hope was that someone would find the dog, and after viewing the information on his identification collar, return him to his rightful owner.

After a few days had passed, with still no word of Sam's whereabouts, McPhail decided to make an inquiry with the Lenoir County Dog Warden's office. McPhail spoke with dog warden, Phil Sanders, about the matter. He asked Sanders whether or not he had recently picked up a dog matching Sam's description. Sanders denied apprehending Sam or any other dog fitting Sam's description. McPhail requested that Sanders contact him immediately if he came into contact with any such animal. Sanders agreed to the request, but failed to honor his word.

On March 14th, McPhail received a tip from a fellow town employee that Sanders was seen with a dog matching Sam's description locked up in the back of his truck. McPhail decided to make a second call to the dogcatcher's office. He left his name, address and telephone number with the attendant and again asked to be contacted should any news of the missing dog's whereabouts become evident.

In just a few minutes the attendant who had spoken to McPhail only moments earlier confided with him that her supervisor, Mr. Phil Sanders, had indeed, captured the animal on March 2 and put him to sleep on March 9. She was not sure why Sanders had failed to make contact with McPhail, because, as their records indicated, the dog had been wearing a collar bearing information pertaining to his owner.

Enraged, McPhail made a third trip to the shelter to ask further questions of Sanders and to try and figure out exactly what had happened to his dog. As the story began to unravel, McPhail learned that Sanders had been contacted at his residence early one morning by Police Officer L.J. Smith, Jr. Shepherd, who was known to have a special disliking for McPhail, and any other black person for that matter, captured the dog and placed him in the back seat of his police car. Desperately wanting to conceal his involvement in the matter, Officer Shepherd, in a very conniving manner, told three town clerks, "Ya'll don't see this dog in the backseat of this police car."

So there it was. McPhail learned that, not only had Sanders acted unprofessionally in the matter, but the whole situation was spawned by one of his fellow officers. According to Sanders, Shepherd reported that a dangerous and vicious dog was growling and barking at people out in front of Town Hall. As dogcatcher for the town of LaGrange, Sanders's services were enlisted to capture the animal and put him to sleep. And that's exactly what he did.

But when McPhail checked with the town clerk and other people downtown, his suspicions were confirmed. Sam had not been barking, growling or showing any such signs of vicious behavior. In fact, two of the ladies working at Town Hall had patted the animal on the head and had admired his friendly. disposition and good behavior. McPhail knew that had Mr. Sanders been honest about the matter and contacted him upon first acquiring possession of Sam, his beloved animal would never have been killed. As a result of Sanders's treacherous actions, McPhail filed charges against Sanders and assumed that the Town would discipline Officer Shepherd accordingly.

The issue was brought before the Town of LaGrange Council members, and while it seemed to McPhail that he had an airtight case, when the matter was put to vote, the result was a 4-2 verdict in favor of the defendant. Therefore, no disciplinary action was taken.

While McPhail, a black citizen, had unwavering evidence and eyewitness testimonials on his side, they were not enough to outweigh the solidarity of the "good ole boy" system that unified the county and the unique way of enforcing the unwritten laws of the land. Sanders was allowed to go free without suffering any consequences for his actions and Officer Shepherd received no form of reprimand by supervising officers or members of the Town Council.

Honor Student Killed

At the age of 17, honor roll student and LaGrange resident Boyd Evans seemed to have everything going for him. He was hard working, bright and personable. But when he is met late one night by a racist police officer, Bobby's prospect of a bright and promising future is lost in the trail of blood that seeps from his lifeless body.

In the fall of 1954, while walking home from work one night, honor roll student and high school senior Bobby Joyner's life came to an untimely end. According to the police report, Bobby was caught peeking through the window of a white female resident. Police shots were fired at the alleged perp and, unfortunately for Bobby, one of those shots proved to be fatal.

The events that chronicled Bobby's death, according to the police report, seemed suspicious to many of the black residents at the time in which they occurred. A trail of blood was found beginning at the lady's residence and ending at LaGrange Elementary School. Residents suspect that the white police officer had encountered Bobby late that evening on his way home from work. The confrontation between the young black boy and the racist police officer grew tense. When Bobby turned to walk away, the police officer shot and killed him right on the grounds of the elementary school. The police officer then enlisted the assistance of a trusted town employee, and together the two of them drug Bobby's lifeless body from the school to the location where he was found beneath the woman's window.

Several years later, the town employee who had assisted with the coverup of Bobby Joyner's murder became ill. It was at that point that he began to fully divulge the facts that outlined Bobby's death and the assistance he had provided in the matter. Unfortunately, the officer who had committed the crime was dead by then and there was no way to bring justice or closure to the case.

Convenience Store Shooting

Many people are hesitant when it comes to working at a convenience store, and rightfully so. On average, each year in America there are more employee deaths and robberies in convenience stores than in any other public location. But, in a 1993 convenience store shooting, the cashier was the one pulling the trigger.

Scott Parker, a white citizen, worked as a cashier at a local convenience store in LaGrange in 1993. One night, during his shift, a black male patron entered the store and attempted to purchase a sandwich. Parker, being the racist and indignant individual that he was, refused to wait on the customer and ordered him to get out of the store. An argument ensued and the customer turned to exit the premises. As he (the customer) turned to leave, Parker reached under the counter, pulled out his gun and fired. The shot hit the customer in the back and he landed face down on the ground.

Mr. Parker, who had a history of being a racist and making derogatory statements against blacks, argued that the black patron had come into the store and had attempted to rob him. Although Parker was not supposed to have a gun in his possession, nor on store property, he was not charged with committing a crime and the citizen's wound went unpunished. The state trooper who arrived on the scene seemed to share Park's views regarding African Americans, being quoted himself by saying, "I hope this guy dies. I hope he dies."

The victim was hospitalized for several weeks, at one time not being able to walk at all. He ended up having to undergo surgeries to correct the problems associated with the back wound. Black citizens became enraged and began to riot. Several shots were fired at the police cars near the incident and bricks were thrown through windows. However, none of these riotous tactics proved useful in avenging the black citizen's injury, or in bringing Scott Parker to justice.

A Frightening Homecoming

After spending fourteen grueling hours behind the steering wheel of his compact luxury vehicle, sleep. rest and solace were the only three things on Lance Corporal Desmond McPhail's mind. But when two LaGrange police officers followed McPhail home, freedom and survival became issues of greater concern.

On April 14, 2002, at approximately 4:00 a.m., Desmond McPhail and his cousin Carl Parker were returning to Desmond's father's home in LaGrange from a trip to South Beach, Florida. Exhausted from driving all night and most of the previous day, the two cousins were anxious to get home and indulge themselves with some much-needed rest. But, unfortunately, upon their return to LaGrange, rest, peace and solitude were the last few things that they found.

When McPhail, the driver, turned onto Caswell Street, he met an oncoming police car. McPhail began to feel somewhat apprehensive because he had heard stories from other local residents about police officials stopping and harassing black motorists late at night. Just as he had suspected, the police car turned around and began to follow the young men home.

McPhail turned into his father's residence, parked the vehicle and went to the trunk to begin unloading his luggage. Just then, Officer Moyer, who had followed McPhail into his driveway, exited his vehicle, pulled out his gun and ordered McPhail to get down on the ground and to keep his hands behind his back. McPhail reluctantly followed the command, but questioned Moyer's reasoning for such harsh tactics. Officer Moyer stated that his request was standard procedure. He then proceeded to handcuff McPhail and placed him in the front seat of the police car. When McPhail inquired about the charges, Officer Moyer stated that he had suspected him of DWI (Driving While Impaired). McPhail questioned how Officer Moyer had come to that suspicion, but Moyer made no attempt to respond to that question. He went on to say, "I could get you for failure to stop for a blue light."

"What are you talking about?" McPhail questioned. "You didn't turn your lights on until you had stopped in my backyard."

To this statement, no reply was made.

After about twenty minutes of being handcuffed and interrogated by Officer Moyer, Desmond's father came out into the drive to see what was going on. At that point Officer Moyer removed the handcuffs from McPhail's wrists and asked to see his license and vehicle registration. Taking the materials back to his vehicle, Officer Moyer proceeded to write out a citation, which he then issued to McPhail. Both father and son found the handwriting on the citation to be illegible and implored Officer Moyer to explain the charges. Moyer refused to explain the charges and would not divulge either his name or his badge number to the pair. However, Officer Moyer did go on to say that if the two would like to file a complaint about him or the citation in which he had issued that they could do so with either the mayor or the town manager.

A few hours later, when daybreak had arrived, McPhail, his son and nephew visited the mayor at his home and argued their case about the unprofessional and unwarranted treatment they had received at the hand of Officer Moyer. McPhail asked that the video of the incident be pulled in order to clear up the matter. The mayor refused to have the tape pulled or viewed by the angry citizens. Finding no relief with the mayor, McPhail was forced to enlist the professional services of an attorney to have his son's name cleared.

When news reporters caught wind of the case, they began to inquire about the footage from the video. The Chief of Police told local news media that the footage in question had been recorded over. Thus, to date, there are no pieces of material evidence pertinent to the case. Not only was McPhail humiliated and inappropriately charged, but he also lost time at work, along with wages fighting to clear up charges for which he was wrongfully accused.

Under the Scooter

Larry Gray had used a scooter as a source of transportation for many years and never once worried about safety. But, in May 2005, his level of confidence and feelings of security were shaken when his scooter collided with the underside of a police car.

On the evening of May 28, 2005, Larry Gray was riding his scooter down Boundary Street. Upon reaching the corner of Boundary and Walton Street, Gray was stopped by Officer Derrick Carter. Officer Carter asked to see Gray's license, knowing fully well that a license was not needed to operate a scooter. Gray questioned Officer Carter's true intent for initiating the stop.

"What's your name?" Officer Carter demanded. "Have you been selling drugs?"

"No," Gray replied. "I don't have to take this kind of harassment."

When Officer Carter seemingly had nothing else to say or any particular reason to detain him, Gray replaced his helmet, restarted his engine and continued traveling down Walton Street. But before he could reach the stop sign at the corner of Spring Hill and Walton, Officer Carter collided with Gray and his scooter.

Thinking that the officer's intent was to kill him, Gray managed to pull himself from underneath the scooter and to hop away to find help. Gray was then transported to the Lenoir County Hospital, where he received treatment for cuts, bruises and a fractured foot. The scooter was towed to a local garage. The mechanic's assessment of the vehicle revealed a considerable amount of damage as a result of the collision. Charges have been filed against Officer Carter, but to date there have been no forms of repercussion taken to rectify the matter.

Pain in the Back

Having undergone back surgery and embarking upon the painful road to recovery, Larry Walton was certain that the worst was behind him. But, when he was forced into an aggressive encounter with the local police chief. Walton's road to recovery veered off to a path in need of much construction.

On September 18, 2003, much of southeastern North Carolina was inflicted with powerful winds, averaging in speeds more than twenty-five miles per hour, damaging hail and severe flooding in some areas, as a result of hurricane Isabelle. The city of LaGrange, like most other cities in the hurricane's path, suffered telephone and power outages. In order to curtail criminal activity, and as an added safety precaution for residents, a curfew was imposed requiring residents to be in their homes, if at all possible, by 9:00 p.m. But, without the aid of electricity, some of the residents were unaware of the imposed curfew. Larry Walton was one such resident.

Just days before the hurricane hit, Walton had been released from the hospital and was at home recuperating from back surgery. In order to help progress his recovery along, Walton's primary care physician had instructed him to walk for an extended period of time each day.

Unaware of the imposed curfew, Walton left his home around 8:45 p.m. and began walking toward the home of one of his friends to see how he had fared during the storm. About midway into his commute, Walton's therapeutic walk was interrupted by LaGrange Police Chief Jim Sutton, who didn't seem at all pleased with their encounter.

"What are you doing out here this time of the night? Don't you know that there is a 9:00 curfew?" Chief Sutton questioned.

"No, sir. I didn't know." Walton replied.

"Don't you get the paper?" Sutton continued with his line of questioning.

"No, I do not," came Walton's second reply.

Chief Sutton studied Walton's face for a moment with an annoyed gaze and finally instructed the pedestrian to get in the backseat of the car. But, knowing that getting in and out of a vehicle could possibly cause more harm than good, Walton declined the chief's offer for a ride home.

"I just had back surgery," Walton explained. "It's difficult for me to get in and out of cars. My doctor told me that I should walk and avoid riding in cars for the time being."

At that point, Chief Sutton became extremely annoyed. Stepping onto the sidewalk, the chief grabbed Walton by the arm, thrust him into the back seat of the patrol car and escorted him home. By the time Walton re-entered his home, the pain in his back had become unbearable. Walton's wife was forced to transport him back to the hospital, where he received additional treatment for the damage suffered at the hands of an irritated and disgruntled police chief. As a result of Chief Sutton's harsh treatment, Walton's back problems were intensified, and he was placed on permanent disability. It has been recommended by doctors that Walton undergo a second surgery to his back in an attempt to correct some of the problems resulting from his damaging encounter that evening with Chief Sutton.

Choked and Bound
The police station is one the last place that a person would expect to be assaulted, but two LaGrange locals found out otherwise.

Terrell Brown and his friend Sam Shaw walked into the LaGrange Police Department one afternoon in 1996 to visit one of Terrell's cousins. Terrell knew that his cousin had been brought into the station earlier that afternoon due to assault charges and wanted to find out if and when he would be released.

When the pair approached the officer on duty and told him the reason for their visit, the officer refused to offer any information pertaining to the arrest and instructed both Brown and Shaw to leave. An argument between Brown and the officer ensued, and, as Brown attempted to leave, the officer grabbed him by the collar, pulled him from the moving vehicle and slung him to the ground. Although Brown was then handcuffed, the arguing continued. At that point, a second officer arrived on the scene and slammed Shaw onto the hood of the car. With seemingly a loss of patience, the first officer reached his hands out, fashioned them securely around Brown's neck and proceeded to choke him until it became noticeably apparent that Brown was struggling to breathe.

Brown and Shaw were detained at the police station for nearly an hour before they were finally released. Shortly after his release, Brown filed a complaint with the town manager, but the town manager refused to act upon the matter. A second complaint was filed with the District Attorney's office. which then forwarded the case to the State Bureau of Investigations (SBI). The SBI investigated the incident, and even after the third officer on the scene attested to the validity of the choking claim made by Brown, the officer was found, NOT GUILTY.

Trade-Mart Brawl

When Larry Gray stopped at a local convenience store to fill his tank and purchase a beverage, he ended up leaving with a whole lot more than he had bargained for.

On the evening of October 14, 2005. Gray entered Trade-Mart Convenience Store. Upon entering the store. Gray noticed two local police officers leaning against the wall and drinking a cup of coffee.

Officer Dixon approached Gray and chided, "You know there's a warrant out on you."

"Yeah? Let me see the paperwork." Gray replied.

Since Officer Dixon made no attempt to produce the "alleged" documentation, Gray turned to walk away. In what seemed like a flash, Officer Dixon pushed Gray in the shoulder, threw the remains of his hot coffee onto Gray's chest and punched him in his right eye. Officer Dixon then applied handcuffs to Gray's wrists and escorted him outside the store where he proceeded to illegally search Gray's person.

As a result of Officer Dixon's abrupt and harsh treatment, Gray suffered a swollen eye, blurred vision and a permanent scar on his chest due to the severity of burns penetrated by the hot coffee. Because of Gray's diabetic health issues, the burns and scarring took months to heal. Not only was Officer Dixon's course of action unwarranted, it can also be deemed as abusive and calculated forms of harassment that need not go unpunished.

Inappropriate Search
Could it be lawful for a male officer to search the private and most sacred parts of a female suspect? Apparently it is in LaGrange.

Barbara Phillips was traveling down Washington Street in the early hours of the morning on March 16, 2002. Upon making a left turn onto Caswell, she was stopped by Officer Ron Moore and Officer Don Tyler. Officer Moore approached the vehicle and disclosed that the reason that she had been stopped was that she had failed to turn on her left turn signal prior to making her most recent left-hand turn. He then went on to ask for Smith's driver's license.

"I don't have one." Smith confessed.

Officer Moore then instructed Smith to exit the vehicle and requested that she submit to a sobriety test. According to Moore, Smith had failed the test. He then proceeded to search Smith in what seemed to be a most inappropriate way. He pulled, twisted, and shook the front of her bra, making various fumbling gestures to the breast and nipple areas.

Once the search had been completed, Officer Moore placed Smith under arrest and transported her to Kinston to be processed and jailed. On the way to Kinston, Officer Tyler was dropped off at the police station, leaving Smith to ride, alone, with the officer who had just violated her.

When Smith arrived at the Kinston jail, she immediately reported the incident to Officer Jennifer Carr, a female officer on duty. But rather than provide empathy in the matter, Carr sneered and chuckled as if the incident were quite amusing.

Smith reported that she felt violated on the morning of March 16,2002, as a female and as an African American. According to Smith, had she bee a white female, she most likely would not have been stopped. If so, she certainly would not have been fondled and inappropriately searched by a mak police officer.

No License Arrest

Drug trafficking, attempted murder, armed robbery, larceny and the like are all common crimes that warrant an arrest. But what about driving down the highway in a smoking vehicle or mistakenly leaving your driver's license at another location? Could these actions be considered crimes worthy of arrest? Like most others, Sondra Newton, a resident of LaGrange, would have answered, "No." But one spring afternoon in 2001, she learned, otherwise.

On that particular afternoon, Sondra had been out running errands for her father. When she arrived at her grandmother's house, she noticed that a police vehicle driven by Officer Valerie Kim had followed her into the driveway. Officer Kim approached Sondra and stated that the reason why she had followed her to this particular location was because her (Sondra's) vehicle was smoking.

Kim then went on to ask Sondra for her driver's license. Having traded vehicles with her father earlier that morning, Sondra then realized that she did not physically have her license with her. She had left her wallet and all of its remains in the glove compartment of her own personal vehicle. She explained what had happened and asked the officer to contact the State Driver's License Department to verify that she did, indeed, possess a valid driver's license.

Officer Kim refused to make the call and a negative exchange of words followed. The argument ended with Officer Kim handcuffing Newton and taking her into custody. When they arrived at the police station, Newton requested that the handcuffs be loosened, as they were hurting her wrists.

Again, Kim refused, stating, "This is what we do to people like you when we get them down at the police station. One guy was choked for running his mouth, so you better watch it."

After detaining and harassing Newton for nearly an hour, Officer Kim decided to contact the State Driver's License Office. Newton's claim of having a valid driver's license was verified and she was promptly released from custody, not withstanding the profane and discriminatory statements that Officer Kim hurled her way.

The Non-Speeding Ticket

Sweaty palms and a racing heartbeat are uncontrollable reflexes that are likely to follow when a speeding driver looks into his rearview mirror and sees flashing blue lights. Most drivers know that the flashing lights are almost always indicative of a speeding citation that is sure to follow. But for a person who is driving within the posted speed limits and following traffic guidelines, receiving a speeding citation should be the last thing on the driver's mind. Well, maybe things are different in LaGrange.

At approximately 11:30 p.m. on the evening February 16, 2002, Jake Miller and his daughter Ciera were returning home via Railroad Street.

When Miller turned onto Cary, he noticed blue lights flashing in his rearview mirror. Miller pulled over and Officer Don Tyler approached the vehicle.

"Good evening, sir. My name is Officer Don Tyler. Could I see your license and registration?"

"Is there a problem, officer?" Miller asked.

"The reason I'm stopping you is because you were speeding."

"Officer, I checked my speed twice, before the vehicle in front of me passed you and I was under the posted speed limit both times." Miller explained. "Plus, my radar detector went off, so why would I come by you speeding?"

"Could I see what speed you clocked me going?"

Officer Tyler peered into the vehicle viewing the radar detector atop the dashboard. Perceiving that Miller had called his bluff, Officer Tyler instructed Miller to have a "good night" and bid him safely on his way.

Three Pointless Stops

Up until July 2001, Mark Thomas had had no qualms to speak of with the LaGrange Police Department; however, by the time the month had ended, White had experienced more than his share of negative law enforcement encounters.

Interestingly enough, White was stopped a total of three times without even coming close to breaking a law. And what one might find even more interesting is that each time he was stopped, Officer Don Tyler was the uniformed individual who pulled him over.

The first stop occurred around 5:00pm, right in White's own back yard. As he pulled into his driveway, White noticed that a patrol car had followed him into the drive. White exited the vehicle and made a wondrous inquiry to the officer as to why he had followed him home.

"Well, you did a California Road By," the officer stated.

"A what?" White asked, with a rather confused look on his face.

"A California Road By," the officer went on to explain, "is when a driver approaches a stop sign, slows down, proceeds with caution, but never comes to a complete stop."

Knowing that the officer was following along the path of several streets, White had taken extra precautions to follow traffic laws, rules and guidelines. Failing to come to a complete stop at a stop sign was a traffic violation that he knew had not been broken.

"Officer," White went on to say, "that just doesn't make sense. I saw you following me all the way from Main Street. Why would I run a stop sign knowing that you were right behind me?"

Officer Tyler made no attempt to answer White's question, but rather responded with a question of his own. "Could I see your driver's license and registration? I'm gonna check and see if you have any outstanding warrants."

With that said, Officer Tyler returned to his vehicle and made the necessary checks. In less than five minutes he returned White's articles of driver identification and told him that he was free to go.

A week or so later White was, again stopped by Officer Tyler just as he was entering into his drive. On this particular occasion the officer's claim was that White had swerved while driving. White, again knowing that he had been extremely cautious and careful not make traffic violations while driving, argued in his defense.

After checking his driver's license and vehicle, Officer Tyler released White and told him that he was free to go.

Being stopped twice by the same officer at his residence for seemingly no apparent reason, White began to sense that the stops were pre-calculated and very possibly the seeds of harassment. He decided to go down to the police station and file a complaint against Officer Tyler and his tactics of harassment. White discussed the matter with Police Chief Jim Sutton and requested that the three of them sit down together and have an open discussion about the two unwarranted stops. Chief Sutton didn't think that it would be necessary to have a formal meeting with the officer and the resident, but rather, agreed to look into the matter himself. Whether the chief followed through with his investigation or not is uncertain to White, but what is certain to him is that a few days later, upon returning home from the grocery store he was stopped by Officer Tyler yet again.

Officer Tyler, again, stated that the reason for the stop was due to swerving, but this time wanted to know if White had been drinking.

"No," said White, rather annoyed.

It was obviously apparent that the chief had failed to investigate the harassment complaint that he had filed against Officer Tyler.

"I'm gonna request that you submit to a sobriety test," stated Officer Tyler. "Hold your head back and arms out," Tyler instructed, "and raise your right foot like this." But, with that, Officer Tyler lost his balance and fell forward against the hood of the police car. He's the one who needs to take a sobriety test, thought White, still feeling rather aggravated at the unwarranted series of stops.

As White was preparing to take the sobriety test, a second officer pulled onto the scene and told Officer Tyler that she would handle things from there. Being duly aggravated and disgusted with this third stop at his residence, White confided in Officer Kim and explained to her the acts of harassment that he had endured throughout the past few weeks.

"Officer Tyler is trying to make a name for himself," explained Officer Kim. "Believe me," she went on to say, "you're not the only one that's getting picked on."

LaGrange's Finest

In the early morning hours of February 17, 2002, Linda Keys and her boyfriend, Dennis Whitley, were stopped by two LaGrange police officers for seemingly no apparent reason at all. As the couple turned onto Phillip's Street, they noticed the blue lights flashing in the rearview mirror and pulled off onto the shoulder, unaware and unprepared for the perilous events that would soon follow.

Officer Tyler was the first to approach the vehicle, asking Whitley for his driver's license and to step out of the vehicle. Whitley obliged.

Tyler then instructed Whitley to turn around and face the car.

"Why," asked, Whitley.

But rather than provide a verbal response, Officer Tyler grabbed Whitle by the neck and slammed him face down on the hood of the car. Due to a back- related disability, Whitley was under doctor's care and knew that he could not withstand such harsh blows.

"I'm under a doctor's care," he pleaded, but the officer made no attempt to lesson his blows. Whitley was then slammed to the ground and the officer proceeded to ram his knees and elbows against the suspect.

When Linda saw what was going on, she jumped out of the vehicle and attempted to offer assistance. At that point, Officer Ron Moore pointed his gun directly at Linda's head and snarled, "If you take another step I will blow your fucking brains out! Get your black ass back in the car."

Whitley was then handcuffed and taken into custody. Taking the keys to the suspect's vehicle, Officer Moore directed Linda to get home the best way she could. By then it was almost 3:00 in the morning and Linda's house was more than two miles away. Throughout the duration of that cold and lonely walk home from Walton Street to Springvilla Drive many fears and insecurities began to pop up in Linda's mind. Linda, who at the time, was nearly five months pregnant, feared not only for her own personal safety, but for the safety of her unborn child. That night, two of LaGrange's finest became, for Linda, two of the most feared, and rather than subject her young to the harsh and discriminatory treatment of the LaGrange Police Department, Linda moved well out of their jurisdiction to a town more than fifty miles away.

Drug Zone Targets
On the night of March 16, 2002. Travon King and his lifelong friend Ricky Thomas found themselves in a dangerous encounter with local police officers that almost ended up costing them their lives.

Terry Blount and his friend Erie Thomas had spent most of the evening shopping and hanging out with friends in Goldsboro, a city located about twenty miles west of LaGrange. The young men decided to make one last stop at a local convenience store to purchase cigarettes and a beverage before heading home. But when Terry pulled up to the front of the convenience store and saw a handful of "would be" troublemakers congregating in the parking lot, his desire for a cold drink and smokes subsided, and he decided to go ahead and go home.

As the pair pulled onto Cary Street, Terry noticed that the police car that had been parked along the curb had pulled out behind them. "I think those cops are following us," said Terry.

"Are you sure?" asked Erie, beginning to feel a little anxious. He had heard rumors that local police officers had been stopping black drivers late at night and pulling their guns on them. The prospects of witnessing that rumor become a reality filled his countenance with nothing but pure dread.

"Yeah, I think I'm just going to go ahead and pull over," said Terry.

As the car approached the intersection of Cary and Boundary Streets, Terry pulled the vehicle over to the side of the street. But rather than pull off the street behind them, the patrol car continued a short ways down the street and parked directly in front of Terry's yard.

Still somewhat curious as to what these two police officers were up to, Terry pulled into his driveway and drove up along the side of his house where he customarily parked his vehicle. Not being able to withstand the suspense any longer, Terry walked up to the police car with high hopes of finding out why they had followed him home.

"Is there a problem, officers?" Terry asked.

Making no attempt whatsoever to shed light on their reasoning for being parked in front of his house, the officers redirected Terry's question by responding with a question.

"Don't you know you're approaching a police vehicle? Do yourself a favor and step away from the car."

Terry looked at the officers for a moment with a puzzled look on his face, but he dared not stare too long. Terry knew that he had not broken any laws, but he didn't quite know what to make of the two officers and the fact that they were just sitting stationary in front of his home.

"Hey, man," Erie yelled, standing with one half of his body outside the passenger side of the car, "take me home."

Seeing that he was making no leeway with the officers, Terry obliged. As he turned to walk back to his vehicle, the two police officers drove off.

"What was that all about?" Erie asked as Terry buckled his seatbelt and began backing out of the yard young men placed their arms out the window to show the officers that neither of them posed a threat.

The two officers approached the car, one on either side of the vehicle, and with their guns raised and flashlights shining at high beam, instructed the young men not to move.

"Don't move or I'll blow your fucking head off," one of the officers bellowed.

"I have a gun in the backseat of the car." Terry volunteered. "It's registered."

The two officers didn't seem to be the least bit impressed with Terry's open disclosure of information concerning the gun. Instead, they instructed the two young men to step out of the vehicle and proceeded to place them in handcuffs.

"What's going on?" a woman yelled from the porch. "Erie... Terry, are you okay?" The flashing lights, voices and other noises must have awakened Erie's parents.

"The reason why we stopped these two young men, ma'am, is because this is considered a drug zone," one of the officers began to explain.

"What are you talking about?" Erie interrupted. "This is where I live." Erie's parents corroborated his story. Seemingly, almost as quickly and quietly as they had followed the young men and threatened to end their lives, the two officers returned to their vehicle and calmly drove away. Terry and Erie were shaken, to say the least, and for weeks thereafter wondered what would have happened to them had Erie's parents not arrived on the scene when they did.

The No Warrant Arrest

Based on the verbage found in the United States Constitution. American citizens are considered innocent until proven guilty. But for one U.S. citizen residing in the city of LaGrange, the opposite was found to be true. Not only was he considered guilty for a crime in which he did not commit, but he was also arrested and publicly humiliated without a warrant in place to justify the arrest.

On August 11, 2002, Keven Sapp was arrested and taken into custody by two police officers from the city of LaGrange on charges of failure to pay child support. It was only days earlier that Miller was approached by Sheriff Brown and two LaGrange police officers at a local convenience store. When Sheriff

Brown attempted to make the arrest, Miller explained to him that the charges had been dropped by the district attorney due to lack of evidence. The warrant that had initially been issued for his arrest had been stricken. The sheriff accepted the story to be true, but warned Miller that if he found out otherwise he would personally pursue the arrest. Miller knew that his story was indeed true, so when he exited the store he put matter behind him. But when walking down Washington Street late one evening the matter found a way of re-surfacing.

Officers Carter and Hall had been patrolling the area that evening. Once they seemed to leap at the opportunity to carry out his arrest.

"Keith Miller, you're under arrest," began Officer Carter. "You have the right to remain..."

"What are you talking about? I told you all the other night that the warrant had been stricken," pleaded Miller with a hint of disgust. "Didn't you..."

"We know what you told us," Officer Hall interrupted. "According to Sheriff Brown the warrant still stands."

"Anything can and will be held against you..." Officer Carter continued with the Miranda rights, but Miller just tuned the officer out as he continued to argue his case.

"Well, he must not have checked into it. All you have to do is call Attorney Williams. Donald Woods. And he'll tell you that the warrant is stricken."

"If you can not afford an attorney, one will be appointed to you," Officer Carter continued as if Miller had not said a single word.

En route to the police station, Lenoir County Deputy Sheriff Ellison was met and asked to take Miller to the Magistrate's Office. Deputy Ellison agreed, and Miller was placed in the back seat of her patrol car. Again, Miller attempted to argue his case and express his disdain in being wrongfully accused.

"You'll be able to make a couple of calls," Deputy Ellison responded. "If what you're placed in a holding cell and instructed to wait.

Unfortunately for Miller, a little while turned into a number of hours. It was approximately 3:00 in the morning before his innocence could be confirmed. Miller's story was verified, and he was eventually released. Both the Magistrate and Deputy Sheriff apologized to Miller for the inconvenience that he experienced and for being wrongly accused and arrested. Neither of them could understand why Sheriff Brown or the two officers would pursue the arrest without first making sure that a warrant was in place, nor could Miller. But as time progressed, Miller's understanding of his, "no warrant arrest" became clear. After sharing his story with other African Americans within the community, Miller learned that his arrest was not an isolated incident. He learned that several LaGrange minorities, especially those of color, had been the recipients of racial profiling and acts of harassment delivered by town officials and local police officers. The "no warrant arrest" was not a mistake, nor was it an oversight. It was a callous and malicious act of harassment that had become an all to familiar occurrence for the minority residents of LaGrange.

White or Black: Who's at Fault?

According to experts, there are few, if any, "no fault" accidents involving motor vehicles. There's almost always someone at fault, and that someone, under average circumstances, is issued a citation. But, in the city of LaGrange, two drivers learned that the person ticketed didn't have to be at fault, he just had to be black.

Scene 1
One evening in 1987, Thad Knowles, a LaGrange citizen was traveling along West Boundary Street when his car was sideswiped by a young white female. According to witnesses, the young lady, who had received her driver's license just a few hours prior to the collision, had failed to stop at the stop sign at the corner of West Boundary and Center. She and Knowles entered the intersection at approximately the same time and thus collided.

When Assistant Chief Brook May arrived on the scene, he assessed the damages and spoke with both drivers individually. The girl stated that she had been adjusting the radio station and didn't see the stop sign until it was too late. By the time she saw it, she was going too fast to come to a complete stop. She had attempted to apply the brake when she recognized what was about to happen, but by then it was too late.

Afterwards, a couple of pedestrians who had witnessed the accident approached Assistant Chief May to offer their eyewitness accounts of what had happened. They both confirmed that the young lady had indeed run the stop sign and caused the collision. But when all was said and done, the young white lady drove away emptyhanded, while black citizen Thad Knowles was left holding the ticket.

Later that day, Knowles was approached by the young girl's father, a LaGrange school principal, who offered him a $1500 bribe to take the ticket, pay the fine and keep quiet about his daughter's fault in the accident. Feeling that he had been wrongly accused and unfairly treated, Mr. Knowles sought aid from a local attorney. The attorney obtained sworn statements from the two eyewitnesses, along with body shop assessments and estimates. After reviewing the aforementioned pieces of evidence, the judge dismissed the citation and cleared Knowles' name of all charges.

In all, Knowles lost time away from work and numerous dollars in court costs and attorney fees. But, more importantly than that, he lost his belief in democracy. The day that Assistant Chief May issued him a citation for a traffic violation that he did not commit was the day that Knowles stopped believing in liberty and justice for all.

Scene II
Early one evening in the Fall of 1991, Sharon Miller, an African American female, was involved in a collision with a white business owner, Robert Cavenaugh. Moments prior to the accident, Miller and her son had been traveling along West Railroad Street in the direction of Town Hall. She was caught off guard when the peripheral of her eyes caught a glimpse of Ford and his motorcycle colliding with her vehicle. Miller attempted to persuade her vehicle to veer to the other side and avoid colliding with the motorcyclist, but with the rate of speed that he traveling, a collision was inevitable.

While waiting for the patrolman to arrive, Miller assumed that Ford had failed to look both ways before turning onto the highway. He'll probably get a ticket for this, she thought to herself, and I'll have to file a claim with his insurance company. But when Officer Bob

Nelson arrived on the scene and questioned the two drivers, Miller found that her way of thinking was completely off base.

"I saw the vehicle approaching, but I knew that I could safely enter," Ford explained. "Next thing I knew she was trying to run me off the road."

Officer Miller took statements from both parties, along with methods of contact and other bits of information pertinent to the accident.

"You can come by the police station in a day or two," Officer Miller advised, "to pick up a copy of the report."

From past experiences Miller knew that she'd have to submit a copy of the accident report to the insurance company in order to have her vehicle repaired, so two days later she followed the officer's advice. However, when she arrived at the station, Miller was told that the report had not yet been filed and that she should try back in a day or so. On her return visit to the police station, the accident report was still missing in action. Finally, on her third n obtain a copy of the report. Miller was told that once it was filed, a copy would be mailed to her. Unfortunately, it must have gotten lost in the mail because to this day it has not been received.

In retrospect, Miller realized that the report could not be found in the file drawers of the police station because it had probably never been written. When it came down to it. it was just her word against Ford's, and apparently the wealthy and white business owner had won. Miller, along with many of the other police officers, had allowed race and politics to become the primary factors of influence when deciding how and when to enforce laws, rules and ordinances within the city limits of LaGrange. Like Miller, when race becomes the deciding factor for town management, minorities will always find themselves on the losing team.

A Gift That Keeps on Giving

Most people enjoy being on the receiving end of a gift exchange. LaGrange business owner and land developer John Wynn was no exception. Several years ago town officials presented Foss with the gift of free upkeep and maintenance for the cemetery plots that he sold to local residents.

For more than twenty years, white business owner James Foss has been selling cemetery plots to LaGrange residents. Each time a plot was sold, Foss assured patrons that the sites would be maintained at no additional cost. Sounds like a fair and upright way to do business, right? But unbeknown to his trusting clientele, inadvertently, they'd be the ones footing the bill.

You see, several years ago town officials had agreed to be responsible for the mowing, weeding and general upkeep of the cemetery owned by Foss and his family. The cemetery, which had once been a "For Whites Only" resting place, had always been well maintained. Apparently, local officials wanted to keep it that way. So, in a "behind the scenes" and "under the table" kind of way, the town manager and his staff of elite councilmen agreed to use tax payer dollars to maintain the property. It was likely that the remains of many of their dear loved ones were permanently stationed within the parameters of the Foss cemetery and, undoubtedly, they wanted to ensure that its aesthetically appealing appearance never faltered. And since this decision was reached in a most discrete manner, very few customers realized that they were still making payments on their previously purchased plots, year after year when they paid their taxes. James Foss and the town officials must have decided to keep that tad bit of information to themselves. The public services director of LaGrange has spent in excess of $1,000,000 worth of tax payer money. But, estimated that in maintaining the property for the past twenty years, the town as the old cliché goes, "All good things must come to an end."

In a July 2006 meeting, town officials agreed that they would no longer fund the upkeep and maintenance of the cemetery. They suggested that Foss contract the services out to local vendors. Obviously seeing the plots as liabilities rather than assets, Foss attempted to convince board members to take ownership of the plots, but, unfortunately, he was left holding the bag.

Overworked and Overlooked

In most workplaces, an employee who works hard over a period of time is rewarded with a raise, or at the very least a promotion. That has become the basic expectation for employers and employees around the country. But after working nearly two years at the LaGrange Police Department, Officer Cliff Lawson learned that America's basic workplace expectation was not realistic at all.

Cliff Lawson had more than eight years of experience in the field of law enforcement when he became employed by the LaGrange Police Department. When offered a part-time position, Lawson readily accepted, believing that he would become a most likely candidate for a full-time position when one became available. He worked many long hours to make sure that his work was completed efficiently and in a timely manner, as well as helping other departmental staff when needed.

But, unfortunately, Lawson's plans for advancement or full-time employment with the LaGrange Police Department fell through. A fellow officer reported to Lawson a comment that the chief had spoken to him. According to the officer, Chief Sutton stated that it would be a cold day in Hell before he hired Lawson as a full-time police officer. When a full-time position became available, Lawson would eagerly submit an application packet, but never made it beyond an interview. A white officer was consistently appointed to the full-time positions. Lawson watched this scenario occur five times during the twenty-two months that he served as a part-time officer. It was only when three white officers resigned that the police chief offered Lawson a full-time position with benefits.

The Bogus Ticket

No one wants to be ticketed for disobeying traffic laws, especially when a violation is not committed. LaGrange resident Vick Joyner was no exception to the rule. However, on September 24, 2005, Joyner received a citation for seemingly no reason at all.

Around 7:45 p.m. on a warm September evening, Vick Joyner was in his vehicle traveling along West Railroad Street when he came to a point in the street that seemed as if a sizeable portion of pavement was missing from his side of the road. In his day to day travels throughout the city, Joyner knew that construction had been going on in the area, but for some reason the contractors had failed to place cones around the spot to warn drivers to take necessary precautions. Thus, when he arrived at the disproportionate section of highway, Joyner was forced to dodge out into the other lane in order to avoid wreck or damage to his vehicle. After he had safely maneuvered around the street cut- out, Joyner noticed flashing lights in his rearview mirror. Wondering within himself what could possibly be the matter, he pulled off onto the shoulder and waited for the officer to approach.

"Good evening, sir," spoke the officer, in a rather introductory manner. "My name is Officer Hall. I need to see your driver's license and registration, please."

"Okay," Joyner handed the officer the requested materials. "I haven't done anything wrong, have I?"

"Well, you mind telling me why you were traveling on the wrong side of the road a little ways back?" the officer questioned.

Joyner explained that he was forced to veer onto the other side of the road in order to avoid hitting the hole and causing damage to his car. "I'd forgotten that they've been working on the highway and when I came up on the hole, I had to veer out to miss it."

"Okay," responded Officer Hall. "Wait here, I'll be right back." Joyner sat in his car and waited for the officer to return. He must be calling in to verify my license or checking my tags, he thought.

But when the officer returned, he handed Joyner not only his license and vehicle registration, but a ticket as well. "Sir, I've issued you a citation for driving on the wrong side of the road. The fees and court date are written on the back," the officer stated in a rather monotone sort of voice. "The traffic laws are in place for your safety, as well as for the safety of others," the officer continued. "Have a good night." Leaving those 'warm words of encouragement, the officer returned to his vehicle and drove away.

The next day Joyner returned to the scene, this time with a camera in hand. He took several shots of the massive hole to use as evidence for his defense. On November 15, 2005, Joyner was scheduled to appear in court. Once the District Attorney had the opportunity to review the pictures that Joyner had taken of the scene, the charge was dismissed.

Lights Out, Hands Up

Have you ever been driving down the street for a short distance and realized that you didn't have your lights on? This is something that every driver has probably done at some point and time in his life. But how many drivers have ever been held at gunpoint for such a cause? In the late Fall of 2002, LaGrange resident Thurman Jones found himself in such a predicament.

On the evening of November 2, 2002, Thurman Jones found himself traveling down James Street in the town of LaGrange en route to his home. After turning right onto Hadden Street and pulling into his driveway, he was shocked, at best, when he realized that he had been followed home by two police officers. The two officers, Kim and Hall, sped into the driveway just as Jones was exiting his vehicle. With both of their weapons drawn, they ordered Jones to return to his vehicle.

"What's going on?" Jones asked. "What's the problem?"

"Get back in the car!" the officers yelled.

With the fear of being gunned down in his back yard being the most prevalent emotion in his cognition, Jones quickly acquiesced and followed the officers' commands. He sat in his car wondering if this were by chance a case of mistaken identity. That could be the only logical reason to explain the two officers rushing into his driveway and pulling their guns on him in the manner in which they had done.

Slowly and deliberately, the two officers approached, one on either side of the vehicle. Officer Hall looked through the window of the passenger side, while Officer Kim directed his attention toward the driver. The first question that she asked was, "Have you been smoking marijuana?"

"No." Jones replied. "The only thing that I've been smoking is the cigar that you see me with, now."

After completing what seemed to Jones to be a "much too thorough" search of his car, Officer Kim asked to see his license and registration. She explained to him that he had been stopped because he was riding down the street without the use of his headlights. For this reason, (and this reason, alone) she was issuing him a citation. For some reason things didn't seem to add up. It was true that Jones had been riding down the street with only the use of his parking lights. This was a haphazard mistake. Because the street lights had appeared to be so bright, Jones had failed to realize that he had been navigating his vehicle with only the aid of his parking lights. However, this realization still didn't seem to warrant the need to be held at gunpoint. Thus, he questioned the two officers about their unwarranted behavior. "Why did you pull your weapons and hold me at gunpoint?" he asked.

"This is standard procedure in situations like this." came Officer Kim's reply.

"Situations like what?" Jones thought aloud. "Driving down the street without headlights?"

Officer Kim restated her initial response. "It's standard procedure, sir. We were just doing our job." She then handed Jones the citation and bid him to have a good evening.

On the day of his scheduled court appearance, Jones pled his case to the DA. He explained the details of the case and the actions that the police officers had employed. After hearing his argument and reviewing the evidence that had been presented by the Town of LaGrange, the district attorney dismissed the case altogether.

Caught in the Rain

Lying face down in a puddle of mud. with their wrists bound smugly behind their backs was not the scene Terry Blount and Keith Miller envisioned when they decided to wrap up their evening. But with an unfriendly encounter with two LaGrange police officers, that's just the way their evening ended.

On a cool and rainy night in March 2002, Terry Blount, Rod Jones and Keith Miller were traveling through LaGrange. As the trio turned onto Caswell Street, two approaching police cars met them. The officers turned around and followed Blount and his friends onto James Street, where they (the police officers) then turned on their lights and bid the vehicle to pull over. Once the car came to a stop, passenger Rod Jones began to flee on foot. At the time, Blount and Miller were not aware of the pending warrant that had been issued for their friend's arrest. Perceiving that he would be taken into custody, Jones exited the car and ran away as fast as he could. Officer Paul Hall chased the suspect.

At that point, Officer Ron Moore approached the vehicle with flashlight and weapon drawn. He pointed the gun directly at Miller, while Officer Sue Watkins walked around to the driver's side and approached Blount in the very same way. The passengers were then instructed to exit the vehicle, handcuffed and placed face down on the ground.

For nearly thirty minutes, Blount and Miller were made to fear for their lives as Officer Moyer held them at gunpoint and Officer Kelly completed a rambunctious search of the vehicle. Repeatedly, the officers hurled profanities at the suspects and used their positions of authority as a tool for intimidation. Statements such as, "If you move an inch, I'll blow your damn heads off," and, "Go ahead. Give us a reason to kill your black asses," were repeated over and over again to the point that neither Miller nor Blount expected to make it out alive.

As their luck would have it, Officer Kelly's search of the vehicle came up short. She was unable to find anything in the vehicle, or in their possession to warrant an arrest, thus the young men were released and free to go. When asked why they had been stopped in the first place, the only reason reported by the officers was, "Your tags were almost dead."

At the Car Wash

Getting splashed in the face with a bit of soap and water is a logical expectation to have when visiting the car wash, but getting sprayed with mace...well...that's another story.

On a hot summer day in June, 1994, motorcyclists Ronnie Hand, David Martin and Dominique Hill stopped at a local car wash to clean up their bikes. The trio, being the good friends that they were, spent more time talking, laughing and reminiscing than they did shining and buffing their bikes. As the stories grew and the laughs intensified, the time that boys spent at the car wash passed idly away. Before they knew it, a couple of hours had lapsed. Paying very little attention to the faces that came and went, Dennis and his friends were caught off guard when they were approached by Chief of Police Jim Sutton and two of his officers.

According to the officers, they had recently received a citizen's complaint in regard to two young men speeding and spinning wheels down Washington Street. Dennis and his friends assured the officers that it could not have been them, because they had been right there at the car wash for the past two hours. Nevertheless, Officer Allen Turnage instructed Amp and Maurice to come with him. Turnage placed the two young men in the back seat of the squad car and proceeded with his line of questioning concerning their involvement in the hazardous motorcycle-riding activity that had taken place on Washington Street.

Perceiving that his two friends would be taken into custody, Dennis felt the need to contact their families and alert them of the trouble that was potentially brewing with the police department. He started his bike and began to secure his helmet on his head when a second officer, Jimmy Sasser, switched the motorcycle to the off position and pocketed the keys. Officer Sasser looked Dennis sternly in the eye and said, "The chief wants to see you before you leave."

Dennis walked with the officer to where Chief Sutton was standing, assured the chief that he and his friends had done no wrong and asked whether or not he could have his keys returned. Before the chief had an opportunity to respond, Officer Sasser accused Dennis of obstruction of justice as the chief was in the process of questioning the other two suspects. Without the slightest hesitation, Sasser pushed Dennis into one of the car washing stalls and sprayed him in the face with a heavy dosage of mace. He then palmed the can in his hand and used it as a different type weapon to strike Dennis slightly above his right eye. Obviously sensing the need for guided supervision, Chief Sutton yielded his support by slamming Dennis down to the ground. Dennis was then handcuffed, placed in the back seat of the car and transported to the police station.

Once he arrived at the police station, Dennis contacted his father, who came down as soon as he could. When he arrived, Dennis' father saw the pain and anguish that his son was experiencing from being sprayed in the face by mace. He (Dennis' father) asked Chief Sutton if it would be okay for Dennis to go to the bathroom and rinse out his eyes. Chief Sutton denied the request and instructed one of his officers to transport Dennis to the Lenoir County Courthouse, where he would be required to stand before the magistrate.

Luckily, when the magistrate saw Dennis he realized that he needed to rinse out his eyes and gave him permission to do so.

Dennis spoke with the magistrate and told him everything that had happened from the time he and his two friends had arrived at the car was and the sequence of events that had transpired when Chief Sutton and his officers arrived on the scene. He also stated that there were numerous witnesses at the car wash who could attest to his story and the trio's whereabouts for the time that they had spent at the car wash.

When the local NAACP (National Association for the Advancement of Colored People) caught wind of the incident occurring between the three young black motorcyclists and Chief Sutton and his two officers, one of their members paid the chief a visit. The member warned the chief that the charge that was filed against Dennis (Obstruction of Justice) would not measure up enough to justify the way he was treated. In addition, there were several witnesses at the car wash on that particular afternoon that would swear under oath that Dennis and his friends were indeed telling the truth.

Undoubtedly seeing the error of his ways, Chief Sutton agreed to drop all charges against Dennis, providing that he (Dennis) would not file suit against Sutton or the police department. Chief Sutton also asked Dennis to agree to pay any court costs arising from the incident. Not being sure of his rights and responsibility in the matter, Dennis agreed to the chief's terms to bring closure to the case.

Fighting for Justice

For the residential minorities of LaGrange, there seemed to be no end in sight to the discriminatory tactics used and enforced by police officers and city leaders. Every act of mistreatment seemed to be supported by officials, and those that were not supported were pardoned. It seemed to be a lose/lose situation. Take it or leave it.

But when adversity knocks you in the face one time too many, and you realize that you just can't take another blow to your head, you have a choice. You can either regain your composure and walk away, or roll up your sleeves and fight. I chose the latter. After hearing so many disturbing tales from friends and relatives and seeing my wife and children themselves become prey to the jaded system, I just couldn't take it any more. I had to do something, if not for me, for them.

On January 6, 1997, I spoke out at a town meeting about the serious problem revolving around black citizens and the LaGrange Police Department. The first incident that I reported stemmed from a traffic accident involving my son at the corner of James and Caswell Street. Due to the high volume of traffic in the area, it was difficult to see approaching vehicles (this is common knowledge to the residents of LaGrange). As he was attempting to leave, he was sideswiped by an oncoming vehicle. When my son went to the police station to get a copy of the report, Chief Sutton, not being anywhere in sight at the time of the accident, explained how everything happened. My son's statement was totally disregarded and Chief Sutton filled in the report just as he deemed appropriate. In so doing, the report involved numerous discrepancies, that when asked, he (the chief) could not explain.

I then felt compelled to report the slanderous statement made by Chief Sutton to a junior member of our community. When the young boy went to the police station to report that his bicycle had been stolen, the chief's response was, "You stupid ass! You shouldn't have left it in the yard." When I asked one of the councilmen how he would feel if that had happened to his grandson. he simply answered, "I wouldn't feel too good."

That night, more so than ever before, I felt a deep conviction to lay everything on the line. I wanted council members to know what type of people were enforcing the laws in our community. I remembered hearing about the statement Chief Sutton had made to one of his officers-the statement that "all stupid ass niggers ought to burn." And when asked, under oath, whether or not he had made the statement, the truth about his character came to light when he failed to deny making the racist remark.

I even reminded them of Chief Sutton's pursuit to convict a black man of a double homicide and have him sent to the gas chamber. He had gone so far as to falsify documents pertaining to the case to have the man convicted. Once his wrongdoings were disclosed, his excuse in making the errors was attributed to mistaken identity. In the words of Chief Sutton, "all niggers look alike."

I knew that other black residents shared my level of displeasure with the police chief and most of his officers, and that night I had more than enough ammunition to speak out against them. I went on to tell about Marvin, one of the police officers who I knew personally. I divulged the fact that he had used his rifle to hit a black male in the eye, leaving a permanent scar and had been overheard by more than twenty-five residents calling a blind African American female a "blind nigger." What was the legality of those actions?

Having reported all of the racist acts and discriminatory deeds that I could think of, I felt that the chief's callous attitude and standards of bigotry spoke for themselves. I hoped with every fiber of my being that the council members would force the chief to resign and have the entire police department overhauled. For me, that would be the only sure way to turn things around and establish a feeling of security and continuity throughout the city. But, to my dissatisfaction, and the great dismay of others, there was no form of chastisement rendered to the police chief or any of the members of his department. Business just went on as usual.

Once it became apparent that the mayor and other city leaders were not going to act on the complaints that were being filed, I remembered a lesson that I had learned in grade school. My history teacher, Ms. Henry, made the statement more times than one, "The pen is mightier than the sword." I felt that if my personal pleas to the mayor and councilmen were not enough to warrant a response, maybe I could spark some interest from local residents by having the events publicized. I continued to write letters to the mayor, but also to the district attorney, senators and North Carolina state representatives. I wrote letters to the editor of the Weekly Gazette to be published in the local newspaper and urged others to do so, as well. I wanted anybody and everybody to know how the police chief and his officers were allowed to treat minority citizens. A few other residents decided to publicize in letter format their outlandish encounters and bodily assaults suffered at the hands of local law enforcement. One resident, not only described her unfavorable encounter with local authorities, but she also went on to disclose other incidents of slanderous statements made by white officers to black suspects and the unprofessional conduct demonstrated throughout the department.

On February 17, 2002, Donald White, a citizen of LaGrange and I were stopped between Phillips and Walton Street at around 2:30 am by Officers Tyndall and Moyer. Officer Tyndall asked Donald, the driver, for his driver's license. After Donald cooperated with the officer, he then came back and asked Donald to step out of the vehicle. Once he was outside of the car. I then saw Officer Tyndall slam Donald onto the hood of the vehicle, then throw him to the ground. I then asked what was going on. At that time, his partner, Officer Moyer, pointed his gun at my head and stated, "If you take another step. I will blow your f**king brains out. Get your black a back in the car!"

As a woman, I felt like I was talked to and treated unprofessionally by the officers. Being that I was pregnant at the time, I feel as though my life and the life of my unborn child were threatened.

After, the arrest of Donald White, the Officers Tyndall and Moyer took the keys to the vehicle and I was left to walk home from Walton Street to Springvilla Drive; which is around two miles and it was about 2:40 or 2:45 in the morning.

After being told the information of a town meeting which took place on January 6, 1997, by a citizen that recorded the meeting, it has become my understanding that the town manager and town councilman were knowledgeable of Chief Jim Sutton's discrepancies such as: Falsifying an automobile accident report, drawing his weapon on an African American citizen who was running from him and firing the weapon at the citizen more than once, and then stating to the man when he was later caught. "If you had fallen backwards instead of forward when I was shooting at you, I would have filled your a** full of shots."

In another incident, he stopped an African American drew his weapon and stated, "Hold it right there, you son of a b****h." To add, a Lenoir County Deputy Sheriff witnessed the incident and stated that Chief Sutton was very unprofessional, not to mention all of his improper law enforcement was forced upon the wrong person. To conclude, the LaGrange town manager and some of the town councilman support Jim Sutton in all his racial activities.

This residential outcry against the LaGrange Police Department and Police Chief Jim Sutton's unprofessional and racist tactics spawned a wildfire throughout the community. Most of the black citizens who read the article became enraged, or, at the very least, leery of the police department's discriminatory and abusive practices and the support that it received from the mayor and other town leaders. With the thought that they could become victims of harassment at any given time, many minority residents were hesitant to ride alone in their vehicles, or drive through the city late at night, or in the early morning hours. In an April 2002 Weekly Gazette article, one resident was quoted with the following statement:

"Many black citizens are scared to drive at night because they're afraid they'll get harassed...in the Marines, I'm out there defending my country, but there's a war going on in my back yard."

The lance corporal who made that statement was not far from the truth. For the past twenty years, race relations throughout the community had been somewhat tense, and in the most recent five, they'd grown progressively worse. Black motorists were being stopped for no apparent reason. Some were even being harassed in their own back yards. On one particular occasion, a black male was sitting in his back yard consuming an alcoholic beverage when Officer Valerie Kim drove by. When she spotted the resident seated and drinking in his back yard, she slowed her vehicle to a stop and ordered him to pour out his beer; otherwise she would ticket him for having an open container. Knowing that her threat was totally unwarranted, the resident refused to comply, but questioned her reasoning for issuing the threat. The officer simply stated that she had a gun and a badge and the courts on her side, and when it really came down to it he had nothing.

Undoubtedly, many of the white citizens were oblivious to the scare tactics and discriminatory practices being imposed on the black residents of LaGrange. There lives had not been altered in any way, nor had there been any reported incidents by whites of assault or abuse by police officers. They had not been victimized, harassed or ticketed without a cause, so to them, the police department, chief and town leaders must have been doing an exceptional job. After all, the streets appeared to be a safe haven for residents.

Not only was one white citizen oblivious to the demeaning struggles and abusive practices being endured by blacks, but she seemed to view their outcries as excuses for their wrongdoings and as little more than blatant lies. After reading a series of unfavorable newspaper articles and hearing about the descriptive complaints being filed against the police department by black residents, she obviously felt compelled to render support to the officers and vouch for their upstanding character. In a May 2002 article of the Weekly Gazette, she wrote:

As a concerned citizen and resident of LaGrange, I felt it necessary to speak up on behalf of the LaGrange Police Department, after recent allegations of racism against them. I have had a chance to get to know the law enforcement officers in LaGrange on a professional and personal basis. I ran a business for seven years in the Town of LaGrange and not once did I see an officer, white or black, use excessive force or act any differently toward a suspect based on skin color, they ALL went out in cuffs! And I had ample opportunity to see them in action, with shoplifting and internal theft by employees in my place of business.

To say that I am outraged is an understatement. Officers can't do their jobs these days for fear of someone screaming racism! And this goes for officers of color as well as Caucasian and Hispanic officers. It seems reasonable to me that this officer felt inclined to pull his gun. Think about it. you've observed someone driving left of center...a possible drunk driver...then you have one suspect get out of the car. one in the car, and one officer...and what was the lighting like in this back yard? Stats show that more law enforcement officers are killed in the line of duty at traffic stops than in any other situation! Given the stats, the same situation and set of circumstances. I believe I would have done the same thing. And, it wouldn't have mattered as to whether they were Caucasian, Hispanic, African American, etc.

With young Mr._____ being in the Armed Forces, the fact that one of his family members used to be the Assistant Chief of Police and then a fellow police officer in LaGrange, that he would know, you stay in your car and place your hands where they are visible to the officer. With that and the education of the news media and other advertising agencies, why in the world did young Mr. _____ get out of his car? Now, as to his statement. "In the Marines, I'm out there defending my country, but there's a war going on in my back yard." My father served twenty-eight years in the USMC and fought in the Vietnam war. I have a son that has been actively serving this country for nearly seven years, and as for this crap of a war going on in his back yard...THERE IS NO COMPARISON! I'd like to ask this young man if he's actually seen live combat? I also can't help but ask the question, "If this identical situation had happened and it was a black officer that had done this would we even be hearing about it?"

Now, we wanted LaGrange to become more up to date on equipment, trained officers, even drug dogs, and we have. But, when the resources are used, there are citizens that think they are being harassed. Police officers are always wanted when they are needed, but when not wanted. because of illegal activity, they are said to be harassing people. No one is above the law. If you are breaking it, it doesn't matter what your community status, color, religion, or gender, you must suffer the consequences.

All said and done, I believe that he LaGrange Police Department, as a whole, works hard to make ALL citizens feel safe in their community. I'd like to take this opportunity to say, "We have a very professional and distinguished police force in LaGrange." THANKS AND KEEP UP THE GOOD WORK!

As evidenced in her letter to the Weekly Gazette editor, this particular resident had nothing but rave reviews for the police officers of LaGrange. As a resident and even as a business owner, the officers came to her aid more times than one, and in each and every one of her encounters with law enforcement authorities, she seemed to be duly satisfied. After making her compelling claim of support, the resident lashed out against the Marine Lance Corporal, attacking both his character and credibility. It is evident that she awards very little merit to his account of the events that occurred (i.e. being followed by police and having weapons drawn against him for no apparent reason) and is in many ways insulted by his complaint. It was apparent that this particular resident felt confident in the level of professionalism demonstrated by police officers and supported their actions, wholeheartedly. But how was it that she felt justified in speaking for all citizens, especially those of color?

After reading the article, I couldn't help but think of the many people who had been harassed, ridiculed, embarrassed, and victimized by local police officers. The first person that came to mind was seventy-two-year-old Lonnie George, who had lost his life at the hands of a negligent and uncaring police officer in 1981. Even in his mentally distraught state, I could see him fighting for his life, but when he looked down into the barrel of Officer Basden's gun, his effort to survive became null and void. If his ghost could speak from the grave, would it concur that the "LaGrange Police Department, as a whole, works hard to make ALL citizens feel safe in their community?"

I thought about Thad Knowles and Sharon Miller, the two African Americans who had been faultless in traffic accidents involving white citizens, but they themselves were the ones who were ticketed. I wondered if they would be willing to pledge their undying support for the police officers of LaGrange.

Or what about, Cliff Lawson? Surely he could attest to the attitudes and happenings of the local police department. After all, he spent nearly two years working alongside other officers and under the direction of Chief Sutton. Knowing that he had been passed over time and time again for promotions that were awarded to less qualified and less tenured white officers, did he become outraged with the resident's cry of racism?

Without a doubt, it's easier for a person to become desensitized to events and circumstances that seem to have little or no relevance to their own personal situations than it is for someone who has actually experienced the struggle. In comparison of the two letters previously mentioned, the first writer could be viewed as a victim, while the second, in direct contrast, a victor. They can each testify to what they know to be true about their personal experiences with members of the LaGrange Police Department. The black citizen was harassed, insulted and verbally abused, while the latter, a white female, received professional and courteous treatment every time she needed help. It's no mystery to why their opinions must have differed when it came to matters concerning local police practices.

As our fight continued, with seemingly no domestic support in sight, we decided to seek justice outside of our community. My son, the aforementioned lance corporal drafted a letter and addressed it to the Attorney General's Office. In it, he explained in great detail the sequence of events and the undue treatment that he received at the hands of a well-trained law enforcement official. A copy of the draft was published in the June 19, 2002 issue of the Weekly Gazette. It read:

Dear Attorney General Ashcroft:

As a young man, I became a member of the US Marine Corps months ago because I wanted to serve my country like many of my uncles, grandfather, and great-grandfather. A member of my family has served in just about every military war dating back to WWI. I took a sworn oath to go and fight for my country wherever the Corps deem necessary to defend our country.

I was shocked to learn recently that a war was going on at home in my community, LaGrange, North Carolina. I was returning home from vacation about a month ago when I was followed home by a town police officer with no reason other than being an African-American man. The officer pulled up to my back yard while I was removing my luggage from my trunk. He got out of his cruiser, placed me in cuffs on the ground, placed a gun to my head and threatened to blow my head off. There was absolutely no reason for the police's action, as I had broken not one law. The officer attempted to show probable cause by manufacturing a charge of "driving left of the center lane." The whole incident was recorded by the cruiser's camera. My father and I went to the mayor's house that next morning and reported the incident. We asked that he investigate the matter and preserve the tape of the incident. He failed to honor our request after providing us with a false promise.

After some inquiries on my own, I learned that two (2) of my cousins have experienced similar incidents by the police department. I filed an official complaint with the offices of the mayor, local district attorney, and North Carolina Attorney General. I know that at least ten (10) complaints have been filed with these agencies. The mayor has attempted to block any type of investigation, as he is afraid that all of his unlawful business activities being run from Town Hall will be discovered. The other two (2) agencies for SBI investigation. Meanwhile, many injustices continue have been slow to intervene or state whether they plan to call to be perpetuated against the African American community.

Without a doubt, my hometown police department has and continues to commit criminal atrocities against the African American community and its residents. The chief has used racial slurs, eliminated all African Americans from the force, condoned racial profiling by his officers. condoned his officers of routinely and systematically pulling their handguns and threatening to "blow the heads off" of African Americans, then destroying the tapes of the incidents to cover up their criminal activities. Many in the African-American community have been robbed of their constitutional rights as provided by the Bill of Rights.

The Town officials that took an oath to serve and protect are the very ones serving and protecting themselves. The town mayor, manager and police chief are caught up in their own self-interest and buddy-nepotism web. They perceive any investigation as a threat to their own conflict of interest and possible criminal activities. These guys are running the town for their own self-interest purpose(s) like cartels figures and have absolutely no interest in protecting the African-American community or deterring police criminal activities against its residents. This matter needs to be addressed now without delay before violence spill over into the streets. It is like a power key and crying out for federal interventions.

The President has declared war on terrorism. I do not believe that he meant that domestic terrorism at home should be excluded. With this in mind, I am asking that the U.S. Attorney's Office intervene upon receipt of this letter. As a Marine. I will continue to train and be prepared to fight and defend our great nation wherever it is determined I am needed to serve. Simultaneously. I need my and my community's civil liberties to be restored and protected at home by federal interventions.

This matter is in need of immediate Federal redress. Thank you in advance for your anticipated speedy response.

This letter was also copied to United States Senators John Edwards and Jesse Helms, Congresswoman Eva Clayton, and United States Attorney Frank Whitney. Letters of response were received from two of the recipients Their advice and findings will be discussed in the following chapter.

Small Wins; Big Losses

Whoever coined the catch phrase, "It's not whether you win or lose, but how you play the game" must have never had the pleasure of experiencing the devastating blows of defeat. For in my battle to obtain racial equality among the residents of LaGrange, the wins have been few and of very little significance. But I have to admit, every single win brought with it a sense of progress and a slight hint of producing a change agent.

In the early '90s I was joined by a group of residents who shared my level of dissatisfaction with the police chief and discriminatory practices being used to oppress local black citizens. Together, we united in an effort to declare a hundred residents marched through the town of LaGrange from Washington March on LaGrange. The demonstration went off without a hitch. Nearly four Street to Frink High school, a span of almost two miles. United in brotherly love, we made our silent and peaceful plea for equality.

White business owners looked out their windows as we marched by, some of them closing their blinds or yelling derogatory statements. Some of the town leaders and prominent members of society clapped their hands as if to yield their support of the demonstration. That was 1993.

The following year, having witnessed the huge turnout and show of support from white and black residents alike, a group of protesters banded together to organize a second march. That year, the number of participants had decreased slightly from the previous year, but for a small town such as LaGrange, the showing was still quite astounding. But, other than establish a among minorities and further publicize the mistreatment of black residents, there was little success to be realized once the march had ended.

Although he participated in the marches and group protests throughout town, my brother Charles had a more pressing personal matter to attend to. After his dismissal from the Police Department in November of 1994, a charge of wrongful termination was added to his lawsuit against the police department. Charles had always been an impeccable person when it came to keeping records. Sometimes, in my opinion, he went a little overboard, keeping papers and certificates of recognition from years long gone. But when it came to his lawsuit, the records that he had kept during his employment with the police department proved to be extremely beneficial. In fact, when his attorney had an opportunity to review Charles' records, he told my brother that he had kept the best records of any client that he had ever worked with.

The biggest obstacle standing in the way of my brother's lawsuit was a federal court judge who had a strong disliking for cases involving claims of discrimination. Charles' attorney had worked under the appointed judge as a law clerk several years back. During that time, the Republican judge, conservative in his views regarding civil rights issues, had instructed him to find errors or discrepancies to get the cases thrown out. It was likely that the judge was still exercising the same philosophy. And in the end, that likelihood proved to be a reality when the summary of judgment was issued in favor of the Town of LaGrange.

For the next few years, race relations and discriminatory police practices remained consistent. After addressing councilmen in the January 6, 1997 Town meeting. I felt reasonably assured that change would soon become inevitable. The statement that I provided for council members, along with the accusations of others, I felt, would be enough to warrant an investigation throughout the entire police department. The fact that Chief Sutton refused to comment on the numerous allegations that were made against him was reason in itself to warrant suspension. But, rather than requesting that Sutton step down from his position as police chief, several of the council members banded together and developed a resolution in support of Chief Sutton.

One of the Councilmen, James Lloyd, was disturbed that I was allowed to attack Chief Sutton's character in open session. He felt that the matter was that I had mentioned in my address was still under investigation. Apparently. inappropriate to come before the council due to the fact that the traffic citation he had been insulted himself by the remarks that I made and felt compelled to defend Sutton's reputation, such as it was. The resolution did everything but sound a trumpet in honor of the chief, making him out to be nothing less than the community's unsung hero. It stated that:

Sutton has demonstrated a deep and genuine concern for the town of LaGrange...and the Town Council and mayor supports his performance of the duties and responsibilities of that position...

When questioned as to why resolutions had not been introduced for other town employees, Lloyd responded with, "Because they haven't been raked over the coals." In answering the question of how the council members would respond to the allegations made against the police chief, Lloyd urged fellow councilmen to sign the resolution as a public show of their support for Chief Sutton. Undoubtedly, to his (Lloyd's) surprise, Mayor Felix Sloan refused to sign the resolution, because prior to the meeting he had no knowledge whatsoever of its existence. Keaton requested that the resolution be rewritten, otherwise, he would not acquiesce to sign. The resolution passed with Ron Sutton, James Lloyd, Bill Winston and Steve Pollock in favor. Sam Crouch and Les Shepherd were the only two councilmen who had the courage and conviction to vote against the resolution in support of Chief Sutton. Although the resolution passed with a 4-2 vote, Mayor Keaton's displeasure in the way the matter was handled and refusal to sign the resolution seemed to be a small win in the battle for racial equality in LaGrange. But when the matter was revisited in following month's town meeting, residents learned that council members had held a secret meeting prior to the regularly scheduled town meeting, in which Mayor Keaton had signed the resolution. Most of the black residents in attendance were deeply sorrowed by the mayor's actions and expressed their feelings of pain and remorse by getting up and exiting the meeting long before it was adjourned. Another major defeat!

The resolution in support of Chief Sutton was not the only devastating blow that I received in 1997. After the reports were made alleging the wrong doings of Chief Sutton and several of his police officers, certain council members attempted to silence me and other black residents from making subsequent claims of racism, harassment and verbal abuse by the police chief or any of his officers. Not only that, but they also attempted to ban community marches and Our cries for reform, several residents and I visited Travis Payne, a Civil Rights Outraged with the underhanded and deceptive tactics being used to silence public demonstrations, as well.

Attorney in Raleigh and discussed with him the legalities of the council member's stance. After we had voiced our concerns and disclosed various details of the racial issues that were mounting in our community. Attorney Payne assured us that the town council could not deny me or any other citizen the right to speak out during a Town Meeting. Furthermore, it would be unconstitutional for council members to disallow black citizens the right to march or peacefully protest. At the close of our meeting, Attorney Payne agreed to send a letter to the Town Manager on our behalf, explaining in detail, the unconstitutionality of their attempts to silence public speakers and to halt organized marches and peaceful demonstrations in the city.

It didn't take us long to realize where the allegiance of the council members rested. Once the resolution in support of Chief Sutton was introduced and signed by the town council, we knew that we would be most likely fighting a losing battle. How could we open their eyes to see the racism that stood just beneath their noses?

One thing that helped to shed light on the underhanded and discriminatory practices commonly executed through the police department was to gain publicity abroad. Once the media from neighboring cities such as Kinston and Goldsboro began to catch wind of our claims of racism and discrimination, they started writing articles and running news segments to raise awareness in their own areas. In an April 2002 issue of the Kinston Free Press, an article, titled, Race Issues Mount, made the front cover of the local and state section. The article's subtitle was, Man says he's victim of "driving while black." JHolt Freeman was the staff writer who began the article with the following introduction:

LaGrange-Several recent complaints about racially-motivated police action have led to an investigation of LaGrange Police Officers Robert Moyer and David Tyndall.

The article went on to explain how black citizens were feeling threatened and how they had become targets for both verbal and physical abuse and other forms of intimidation. The fact that an officer had drawn his firearm on a black resident, detained him for an extended period of time and written and issued an illegible citation was the catalyst that sparked the investigation. When questioned about the department's policy for drawing handguns at routine traffic stops, Chief Sutton is quoted with the following statement:

If an officer, for whatever reason, feels he is in danger, he has a right to take whatever steps necessary to protect himself and that can be a show of force, a weapon, or circumstances that may lead to violence. A lot of officers get killed, and the majority in traffic stops.

Chief Sutton was partially right, but not altogether so. The LaGrange Police Department's Use of Force Policy was not only written as a safety precaution for police officers, but for the protection of citizens as well. Use of force should only be used as a last resort. Through the process of my quest for justice, I was able to gain access to the policy and examine the "necessary steps," as Chief Sutton put it, that an officer could use to protect himself. Such guidelines can be found in Section B of the policy. It reads as follows:

Officers are confronted daily with situations where control must be exercised to make arrests and to protect the public safety. Control can be achieved through advice, warnings, persuasion, or by the use of force. While force may be necessary in some situations, it should not be used except as a last resort. The law specifies under what conditions and to what extent force may be employed in GS 15A-401(d).

A law enforcement officer is the only person entrusted with the authority to use force against another person. Because of the extraordinary dangers inherent in this authority, the law strictly defines and limits its use. The law enforcement officer who wields this awesome authority must constantly be aware of its limitations for his protection and the protection of the public.

Getting killed or assaulted during a traffic stop must have been an issue of great concern to LaGrange police officers at that time, because more times than not, black residents were being stopped and sometimes harmed by law enforcement officials. Perhaps they were not aware of the guidelines Surrounding the Use of Force Policy, or maybe they just didn't care.

My family and I were not the only ones enduring the pangs of an unjust police department. Other residents had told me about similar happenings and had planned to file their own complaints within that same week. Having heard more than fifty different stories from residents who had already been victimized by LaGrange police officials, I knew that a silent epidemic was spreading, and it pleased me greatly to have the media's assistance in publicizing the matter. This was definitely a small win for my team.

Once enough people had filed complaints of mistreatment, harassment and racial profiling, the district attorney's office responded to the by facilitating a formal investigation into the LaGrange Police Department. Out of the eleven complaints filed, all but one alleged being stopped for no reason. During each of these traffic stops, residents made claims of either physical or verbal abuse by officers. In five of the situations, officers pulled their weapons and threatened to kill or cause bodily harm to the claimants. In other situations, physical force was used without cause, resulting in a broken collarbone of one particular claimant.

Jim Brady, district attorney for Lenoir, George and Wayne counties issued a response once the investigation was completed. With all the claims of assault and physical abuse that were made, I was none less than disappointed at his findings. On June 13, 2002, Brady issued a statement addressed to Chief Sutton and copied to the complainants. With regards to his findings, he wrote:

...most of the complaints I received dealt with alleged unprofessional conduct by your officers. These allegations do not subject officers to criminal liability, but would subject them, your Department, and the Town to possible civil liability. The allegations should fall within the realm of an internal investigation.

During his investigation, Brady could not find any evidence of criminal wrongdoing. When the officers had been questioned, they all provided "adequate" reasons for their actions, thus negating our claims. It basically became their word against ours, and in the end, their word won.

Brady went on to say that the claims that were made concerning unprofessional acts by officers, which included use of profanity, confrontational attitudes, stopping cars without a reason and racial profiling were possible grounds for civil litigation. In order to address these issues, an internal investigation had to be completed. But with the estimated cost of hiring an outside agency to perform the investigation being between $20,000 and $30,000, we knew that the likelihood of such an investigation becoming a reality would be slim to none. What a loss!

On September 5, 2002, we received a letter from the Criminal Section of the United States Department of Justice Civil Rights Division. The letter was response to our claims of various patterns of discrimination by local LaGrange Police Force and Government. The U.S. Department of Justice's fadings were similar to those of Attorney Brady.

We have carefully reviewed the information which you furnished. However, we have determined that your complaint does not involve a prosecutable violation of federal criminal civil rights statutes. Accordingly, we are unable to assist you.

With the receipt of that letter, another door seemed to close in our face. However, the respondent did go to say that a copy of our allegations had been forwarded to the Coordination and Review Section of the Civil Rights Division to determine whether the alleged conduct might have violated any noncriminal civil rights laws. In that aspect, there was still hope.

Attitude Is Everything

On August 28, 1963, on the steps of the Lincoln Monument, Dr. Martin Luther King, Jr. delivered his world renowned, "I Have A Dream" speech. In it, he discussed in depth the Negro's rightful claim for justice and equality and his refusal to accept anything less. By signing the Emancipation Proclamation, not only did President Abraham Lincoln grant freedom to slaves, but he also declared that African Americans should therefore after receive equal and just treatment. This right became a guarantee for all black citizens the moment they became legal citizens of the United States of America. But nearly one hundred and fifty years later in the small town of LaGrange, the African American is still not free.

One hundred and fifty years later, the short hand of equality and the long hand of justice for the African American residents of LaGrange have been affixed to a clock in desperate need of winding. To pinpoint the pair of hands that first failed to follow through with the winding process would be a rather fastidious task. Was it the lawmakers who failed to enforce the laws or was it the enforcers like Chief Sutton who failed to abide by them? Was it the underhanded city officials who managed the town outside the boundaries of the law, or was it the victims and their families who quietly accepted the unfair hands that they were dealt?

Whether it was the lawmaker or the law breaker, the official or the victim, the fact remains the same. In order to bring about change in our community, a change must first occur in the attitudes of our people. And being that the town commissioners and police officers are the ones who make and enforce the laws that govern our land, their attitudes and political viewpoints seem to be the most logical starting point to ignite change.

A famous writer once pinned the phrase, "Attitude is everything." And, while I can't honestly say that I agree with the statement wholeheartedly, I will say that it's helped me out tremendously in evaluating the character of quite a few people in my life and understanding the patterns in which they think. For instance, I've always known my parents to be honest and trustworthy people. By possessing those noble attributes, they were, in a sense, prevented from telling lies or from treating anyone in an unfair manner. In a sense, their attitude was the determining factor in nearly every single aspect of their lives.

Attitude can be a useful key in understanding why certain people choose a certain course of action in a given situation, whereas others under similar circumstances would choose an adverse direction to follow. In 1994, during my brother's lawsuit for Equal Opportunity Employment, sworn depositions were received from several members of the Town Management committee. Attorney Gilbert S. Rhodes questioned those people, who, in his opinion, had the greatest impact on my brother's case, and being that the suit centered around claims of discrimination and racial injustice, a lot of sensitive questions had to be asked. The responses given to the questions that were posed shone a flashlight that refracted light deep inside the crevices of the witness's character. Among the witnesses selected were Police Chief John L. Sutton, Town Manager Mason Wynn, Mayor Clyde Peterson and various other board members and town employees. When I finally had an opportunity to read the depositions for myself, I have to admit that some of the responses caught me a little bit off guard.

With all of the controversy surrounding Charles' termination from the police department, Chief Jim Sutton and former Chief Ronnie Price's depositions were the first two to catch my eye. And since I knew that Sutton had been one of the key players in Charles' termination, I decided to read his testimony first.

One of the first things that I noticed about Sutton in reading his deposition was that the responses that he gave were very vague, almost in a non- commitment type format, using phraseology such as, "not that I recall" and "not to my recollection." In one particular situation, the attorney shared with Sutton a physician's statement, labeled Plaintiff's Exhibit Number [23]. The attorney presented a copy of the statement to Sutton and read the contents, aloud, assumable to prove a point. When asked whether the note said anything other than what the attorney had read, Sutton's response was, "I can't say that because I can't totally make it out. It appears that's what it says, but I'm not going to say that." After further reading of the deposition, it became apparent that Sutton didn't want to award merit to the doctor's statement because his claim of never before receiving the item had been the grounds for which he had recommended my brother's termination from the police department.

In addition to the non-definitive responses that he gave, Sutton appeared to also be oblivious to the way the police department had been run or the controversy surrounding it prior to his appointment as chief in December of 1993. That was one of the things that surprised me the most. Here is a man who applies, interviews, and accepts an appointment to a position at a police department "under construction." The former chief had been encouraged to vacate the position. The titles of every single police officer had been stripped down to the level of a patrolman. An Equal Opportunity Employment lawsuit had been filed against the town, but specifically against the police department. And, to top that off, the person filing the claim was his direct subordinate. Yet, he knew nothing about the police department or the past records of the employee filing the claim against him and his department. Chief Sutton's responses told me one of two things; either he had spent the past couple of years residing on a planet other than Earth, or he was auditioning for the title of, "World's Greatest Liar." The latter seemed to be the most logical conclusion, given the circumstances.

No one in his right mind would take on a position that he knew nothing about, especially in a department that had received as much negative newspaper publicity as the LaGrange Police Department. Not only that, but in his first few months as chief of police, Sutton had facilitated the termination of a thirten year tenured police officer, whose prior track record with the department. according to him, was nothing more than a mystery. As a person of authority. serving in a leadership capacity, wouldn't an employee's personnel file be the best place to start when preparing for an evaluation? That would have been my assumption; however, according to Sutton, he had problems with Charles work performance from day one, from the way he completed reports to the way he investigated cases. How was it that Charles, under Pelletier's direction, had been able to manage the entire department? With all of the loopholes and discrepancies in the statements that he made, Sutton's testimony just didn't seem to add up.

Once I finished weeding my way through Chief Sutton's deposition, Chief ier was the next one that I selected. Working in the same capacity and under the same title as police chief, I assumed that Sutton's and Pelletier's attitude about Charles and the police department would be almost identical. However; yet, again, I proved myself wrong.

Early on in his testimony, Chief Pelletier acknowledged the close-knit relationship that he and Charles had once shared. According to Pelletier, Charles became employed at the police department somewhere around 1981. He couldn't be exactly sure of the effective date of employment, but as best he could remember it was around that time. Pelletier further acknowledged that, under his direction as police chief, Charles had been promoted in 1986 to the position of sergeant and in 1988 to the position of Assistant Chief. All of that was common knowledge. Nothing new there. But when Attorney Rhodes started asking questions about the evaluations that Pelletier had completed regarding Charles' work performance, that's when I began to see some of the first signs of discrepancy between the testimonies that he and Sutton gave.

Pelletier stated that he and Charles had had a good rapport for the vast majority of their working relationship. He claimed to have no fault in Charles supervisory skills as Assistant Chief and indicated his approval on the employee evaluation forms that were completed under his supervision. In fact, in each of Charles' evaluations that occurred between the time that he was hired in 1981 and the time that Pelletier resigned in 1993, there was not a single category that fell below "good" or "satisfactory" status.

In addition, when asked to describe McPhail and his work ethics, Pelletier confirmed that he was neat in his appearance and productivity, a loyal member of the police department and an honest individual, as far as he knew. According to the former chief, he and McPhail had shared a lot of the supervisory and overall maintenance responsibilities of the police department. They equitably shared the load when it came to developing schedules and supervising patrol; however, scheduling became an issue of controversy for Pelletier and McPhail when newly appointed Town Manager Mason Wynn came on the scene. In Pelletier's words,

There was a conflict, and if I remember correctly, when it started I don't remember the date it started. I don't remember the month it started. But it seems like when it started, about having a schedule fixed and put on the board to work by Mister Wynn, he would approve it. Then it seemed like if Mister McPhail would fix a schedule, he'd approve Mister McPhail's schedule. So, you really didn't know what schedule you it just started a confusion, just like that. Instead of getting any better, it got worse. I could come in here, he would tell me what I wanted to hear. He'd turn around, he'd tell McPhail what he wanted to hear. And that's what got the whole thing started in an uproar. I'm going to be honest and truthful about it.

Pelletier continued with his description and personal interactions with the town manager.

...he was wishy-washy. He would look at my face and tell me one thing: then he would go to another officer, he'd tell him something different. He'd get in front of the town council, it would be different. So you never knew how to take him from one day to the next. He would tell me what I wanted to hear, and everybody that I would go around and talk with. he would tell them what they wanted to hear.

From what Pelletier had to say of Wynn, honesty and integrity didn't seem to be high ranking elements on his list of priorities. If he was "wishy-washy" in his dealings with police officers, wouldn't he also display the same characteristics in carrying out the remaining responsibilities of his job? Intrigued, I lifted his deposition and searched, frantically, for insight into his character.

According to his testimony, John Mason Wynn took on the position of Chief Administrative Officer for the town of LaGrange in July of 1990. Concurrent with that appointment, he also served as Director of Public Utilities for a short time span. In the position of Town Manager, Wynn was second in command in the hierarchy of the town's organizational structure, supervising numerous departments and answering only to the mayor and the town council. His governance covered a vast proportion of the town's jurisdiction, including the Street Department, the Water Distribution, Sewer Collection, the Water Treatment, Wastewater Treatment, Electric Department, the Cemetery, the Recreation Department, both the Fire and Rescue Departments, and last, but not least, the LaGrange Police Department.

In his reign as the city's first town manager, Wynn was granted an enormous amount of power and authority. He was the chief official for the city departments and served as the primary liaison between those departments and the town council. If there was a problem or an issue of concern in the Sewer Collection Department, per se, council members contacted Wynn to gain his assessment on the matter. Based upon his analysis of a situation, the mayor and other members of the council, made their decisions. As town manager, Wynn exercised a great deal of influence over the way matters were handled and the way major decisions in the town were made. The decision that was made on June 7, 1993, concerning the LaGrange Police Department, was no exception.

On that particular evening, the town council met, and one of the particular items discussed was Chief Pelletier's upcoming retirement. Wynn made mention of the discord that had been brewing throughout the department for quite a while and sought recommendation from the mayor and council as how they wanted the problem resolved. That night, the council decided that the best thing to do would be to begin looking for a new police chief and give Pelletier time to get his retirement in order. In the meantime, all of the supervisors would be stripped of their rank, with the exception of Chief Pelletier. The decision to strip the supervisors of their rank and to support Chief Pelletier's announcement for retirement seemed to please Wynn well. Up until this point, Wynn had been given authority to oversee the day to day functions of the police department; however, he lacked the control. With the removal of Chief Pelletier and Assistant Chief McPhail, Wynn would be the primary decisive agent for the police department for all practical matters, and not just in theory alone.

Wynn spearheaded the selection for the new police chief of LaGrange. In August of 1993, Wynn placed an advertisement for the Chief of Police vacancy. The ad was sent to several major cities throughout the state, including surrounding areas, such as Kinston, Goldsboro, Raleigh, New Bern and Wilmington. Approximately twenty-five applications were received by the council, including that of the former Assistant Police Chief Charles McPhail. The applicant pool was narrowed to ten, and according to Wynn, McPhail did not make the cut. Shortly thereafter, the pool was shortened to five, then to three, and finally closed with the appointment of John L. Sutton to the position.

The town manager and the newly appointed police chief seemed to hit it off, well. Working closely together, the two orchestrated a series of changes in the day to day maintenance and functionality of the local police department. Some of the officers who had worked and gained experience under Chief Pelletier's Supervision were either suspended or encouraged to resign from their positions. One former minority officer, Ted Davis, who had been employed with the LaGrange Police Department for nearly two years, reported to work one night during his regularly scheduled shift to find Town Manager Mason Wynn waiting. According to Wynn, Best's had been moved from third shift to second shift. Because he had failed to report at the newly scheduled time, he was being relieved from his duties with the department. It didn't seem to matter to Wynn that Best had not been made aware of the schedule change. He simply asked for Best's gun and badge and instructed him to vacant the premises. Within less than a year's time, a brand new police department and legal structure was developed and implemented in the city of LaGrange.

In the years that followed, Wynn received numerous complaints from residents and city employees alleging Chief Sutton's prejudice and racist treatment against minorities, but failed to follow through with a reprimand or any formal type of investigation. In a letter written by former police officer, R. David Parker, dated September 6, 1994, racist statements made in regards to one particular incident are disclosed. In his letter, he wrote:

I was off duty and had came in to look over a case file in which I was the investigating officer. This case file concerned a black male who lived in LaGrange. After looking over the "5-page, DA's report," I went to give it back to the Chief to secure it in his files. He was sitting at his desk and Jonas Shaw was sitting across the desk near the wall. I handed the "5-page report" to the Chief to proof my work. He began to ask me questions about this case. After explaining the details of this case, they began to laugh at some of the things they found to be wrong in their eyes. They told me that this case would never stick in court. I just stood there to explain some of the things they had questions about and to remind them this was my first felony case. The chief closed the file, and as he was walking to the file cabinet, he stated that the stupid ass nigger should burn like half of the others in LaGrange. Jimmy Sasser was still seated near the wall and had started laughing at what the Chief had just said. Because I do not believe in talking about other people that way. I turned and walked out the Chief's office.

Wynn's subtle acceptance of the chief's illicit practices and garrulous statements made concerning minorities told me a lot about his own personal character. His support of and close-knit ties with such a person disclosed to me a shared vision and an analogous foundation in attitude. In just a very short time, Wynn and Sutton's relationship grew on both a personal and a professional basis, and the two exchanged favors accordingly. For this reason, the town manager never investigated complaints received against the chief, and the chief remained at Wynn's beck and call. Meanwhile, inequality continued to reign, dissension continued to mount and minorities continued to struggle.

The State of LaGrange

In the decades following Lonnie George's death, I've had an enormous amount of time to ponder over those issues that I feel have made the greatest impact on LaGrange's people, economy, and its culture. I'm proud to say that hurricanes, floods and seasons of disaster are not the only times that I've witnessed the city leaders and citizens of LaGrange band together as one. I've seen some of the great things that can be accomplished when our citizens unite together in support of a common cause, such as the downtown Revitalization Project, which spawned new businesses and expansion in areas once deemed less than favorable and other outreach initiatives.

With the implementation of No Child Left Behind (NCLB) and other educational reform initiatives in the Lenoir County school system, I've witnessed public school standards lifted and seen the benefits reaped by our children. Schools in our county such as LaGrange Elementary and North Lenoir High School, among others, have risen to the challenge of both state and federal legislation, and have thus gained national recognition. In addition, we have built new schools and renovated others to provide our children the privilege to learn and educationally express themselves in a safe environment that is ideal for learning.

In an attempt to protect the Town, police officers and citizens stopped for traffic violations or to render an arrest, an adequate supply of tapes and cameras have been placed in police cars. These tapes can be viewed as an extra security measure taken to protect all parties concerned. In the event of a discrepancy, or a violation between an officer and a potential suspect, these tapes could be useful in dispelling any doubts about the sequence of events that occurred prior to the altercation.

In addition, the once all white police department has hired two black officers. This measure should help cut down on the number of and frequency of incidents involving racial profiling and the harassment of black citizens.

To strengthen our economy, the Town Board and other leaders have undertaken a series of new projects to include a new housing development along Highway 903 and a new grocery store and other businesses in the downtown area. These two initiatives alone have attracted new residents to the area and opened up new job opportunities for many of our residents. In addition, lease contracts have continued to be renewed for businesses that lease property owned by the Town. The Town is able to offset some of its yearly expenditures by using the revenue that is generated through these lease agreements.

Agriculture is still an extremely vital component of our rural society. Travelers passing through our town in late April and early May are welcomed by the mouth-watering sight of tasty and juicy strawberries, and in June, July and August by the unforgettable aroma of tobacco leaves that have not yet reached the age of maturation. At any given time of the year those same travelers might view scenes of horses or cattle grazing and chickens sitting on their nests to roost. These seasonal images have remained true to our community for as long as I can remember, and without the onset of tumultuous storms or other forms of inclement weather, I sincerely doubt that they will ever change.

With the growing awareness of ailments and sicknesses arising from health-related issues, many of our citizens have become increasingly more health conscious. Residents and business owners can be seen walking down Center or Railroad Street at any given time of the day. In addition, a Curves fitness center has recently opened its doors in the downtown area to help LaGrange Women shape, strengthen and better care for their bodies.

Outside of the town of LaGrange, Lenoir Memorial Hospital, located in Kinston, North Carolina, continues to open its doors to help local citizens achieve their healthcare goals. The hospital offers several classes to promote physical health and emotional well-being. Some of the classes offered include Yoga, Stress Management, CPR, Better Breathers and Keeping Track. These are just a few of the many classes offered, with new classes being introduced each year. Class instructors demonstrate how to develop and maintain a healthy lifestyle and encourage participants to make the process an enjoyable and lasting experience.

In President Bush's 2006 State of the Union Address, he spent quite a bit of time discussing the issue of compassion. He said:

Americans are doing the work of compassion every day: visiting prisoners, providing shelter for battered women, bringing companionship to lonely seniors. These good works deserve our praise, they deserve our personal support and when appropriate, they deserve the assistance of the federal government.

I urge you to pass both my faith-based initiative and the Citizen Service Act to encourage acts of compassion that can transform America one heart and one soul at a time.

In many ways, the town of LaGrange mirrors the American image of compassion. Most of the residents, black and white, alike, are good-natured and caring individuals who don't seem to mind lending a helping hand when one is needed. They work many long, hard hours, but still take the time to converse and exchange smiles or a friendly wave to a neighbor, visitor, or maybe just a passerby. The crime rate, which continues to grow in most areas throughout the nation, still remains low in LaGrange. Perhaps the down home atmosphere elicits a subtle form of deterrence and discourages would-be offenders from committing crimes. For whatever the reason may be, the citizens of LaGrange have profited from the low incidence of crime while residents in neighboring cities, such as Goldsboro, Raleigh and Kinston have suffered loss.

These factors have remained true to our culture for more years than I can count and were just a few of the deciding factors that compelled me to make the city of LaGrange my permanent place of residence. But, here I must say that, over the years, I've gained a greater appreciation for the meaning of compassion and grown to understand that it comes in many different forms. It's more than a friendly smile or a wave or even taking the time to help a lost traveler find his way back on course. It's more than the provision of aid to the needy or paying a neighborly visit to someone who is sick or shut-in. Compassion is an undeniable act of sympathy. It is most evidenced when expressed to an individual who is experiencing misfortune, mistreatment or a most unfavorable circumstance.

In hindsight, during the address that I made to the mayor and members of the Board in 1997 in the meeting that caused such great controversy throughout our town, I now realize that I wasn't looking for revenge against the chief, nor did I expect to revolutionize the thought patterns of our town leaders. What I wanted most from the board and what I knew to be the greatest need for my people was a genuine sense of compassion felt and expressed by the mayor and all of the members of the board. Whether they believed what I was saying or not was really irrelevant. I needed for them to show sympathy toward me and my son for being the recipients of a falsified police report and feel remorse for people like Dennis Jones and his two friends, who had been harassed and mistreated by law enforcement officers for nothing more than having the wrong color of skin. As an African American, I felt offended and violated by the chief's racist attitude and use of statements such as, "all stupid ass niggers ought to burn" and "all niggers look alike." These were the exact words spoken by Chief Sutton, but when re-told to the Town Board in a Regular Session meeting, earned me the distinct description of being "out of control." Council members took offence to the dialogue and expressed their level of displeasure in the statements that they made to local newspapers and television reporters.

"People were offended."

"You have the gavel."

That was the comment Mayor Pro-tem Hal Davis made to Mayor Keaton. Apparently, Councilman Nicholas O.N. Brewington concurred with Walton, because he went on record with the following statement.

"I don't think I will sit in this room and listen to that type of diatribe again. At some point you've got to say enough is enough."

And finally, Councilman Scott Morris went so far as to say:

"We learned something that night...that we don't have to sit here and listen to that type of language."

While they probably didn't realize it that night, in writing and signing the Resolution to Support Chief Sutton, members of the Town Board failed LaGrange citizens in doing the work of compassion. Their minds were closed to the obvious. Rather than demonstrating mercy or exhibiting an act of sympathy, board members found a creative way to add insult to injury, causing more harm to their citizens than good.

Over the years, I've found the act of compassion to be both an act of mercy and a serviceable deed. But, even more than that, compassion can be used as a tool for one to educate himself on who he truly is and on what grounds his character was built. In most instances, people are inclined to show compassion toward people and situations to which they can relate. In most cases, a wealthy business owner has trouble showing compassion to a homeless person or to a meager pauper. By the same token, a person who has never been on the receiving end of acts of discrimination would be less than sympathetic in understanding the deep and emotional scars of a person who has been affected by such a blow.

A leader who shows mercy, kindness and allegiance to a select few, lacks the character and internal drive necessary to express feelings of compassion to those experiencing the greatest amount of need. In short, the compassion that I sought from the members of the Board in '97, was not a realistic expectation, because the people who had been wronged, unlike Chief Sutton, were neither the elite nor members of their inner circle. They were names without faces and problems without solutions. I now understand that in order for the council to be able to effectively address the issues of racism and discrimination in LaGrange, the hearts and souls of its members must, first, undergo a process of transformation and learn the importance of being able to empathize with one and with all. We may have lost a few of the battles in the fight for equality throughout the streets of LaGrange, but the war is far from being over. For every racist police officer and city official, there is at least one who is just and fair. For every biased and prejudiced member of the town council, there is one who seeks to promote equality and racial harmony throughout.

In January of 2004, town manager Mason Wynn died and the council selected Police Chief John L. Sutton to be his successor. While Sutton's agenda and personal views in regard to black people and other minorities may not have changed, a couple of the council members remain faithful in their positions and help to keep him grounded. There's clearly no way to avenge the murders of Lonnie George and Eddie Moore, or to make right the wrongs that have been suffered by the residents of color. Time, death and distance have all crept in, over the years, and many of the ones who have committed the offences have either died or moved on: likewise, so have their victims. We are fortunate that the events of the past cannot be relived, only remembered. And for those of us who have been around long enough to have experienced any form of racism or discrimination along the streets of LaGrange, for them, equality is not viewed as a privilege, but rather a necessity. Minorities cannot change LaGrange's past, but they can help to redirect its future. For this reason, I am able to count our losses as gains and our defeats as minor setbacks. The adversity that my family and so many others have experienced, over the years, has made us stronger and wiser in our plight for justice and equality. Our wounds have been painful, and our struggles have been great, but our faith and endurance remain strong. As long as we remain true to ourselves and hold fast to our quest for equality, the fight will continue, and change will indisputably come.

Epilogue

The more I reflect on the events that have occurred during my stay in LaGrange, the more perplexed I become and my soul grows weary with unrest. One question leads to another that leads to another that leads to another. Why did the lady throw rocks at the little black boys and girls who were merely walking down the street? Did she hate them because they were black, or because they weren't white? Did Lonnie George's life have less meaning because he was a man of color? Was Officer Chris Baysden set free because he was white or because he wasn't black?

Some people live by the philosophy, "black or white...it doesn't matter, it's what's on the inside that counts." That frame of thought might hold true in some cities and in some states, but, here in Southeastern North Carolina, in the small town of LaGrange, from what I can tell, color seems to be the only real thing that matters.

When I share some of the stories that I've heard and witnessed on the streets of LaGrange, listeners always seem to stare at me in sheer amazement with eyes stretched wide. Most are shocked to learn of the hatred and corruption that exists among our leaders and the blatant forms of unlawful acts that continue to go unpunished. The discrimination and corruption that should have died out with the Civil Rights Movement of the 1960s and '70s, somehow continues to live on. Today, racism and discrimination are very much alive and well in LaGrange, they've merely changed forms. It's not always easy to spot, and at first glance you'll probably miss it. For onlookers, it can be compared to a beautiful, multi-million dollar house with an interior that has been infested by termites. From the outside, you'd never be able to notice anything out of the ordinary, but after careful inspection you'll see that it's rotten to the core.

Today, black boys and black girls can feel reasonably assured that they will be safe when walking down the streets of LaGrange. They don't have to worry about being the target of racial slurs, or even about being hit by a rock. Young black mothers don't have to worry about sending their son into a department store and having him gunned down if, by chance, he accidentally grazed up against a white female. I'm proud to say that type of racism no longer exists. Today, there reigns a more silent and subtle form of racism in LaGrange that is like none other. Police officers target unsuspecting minorities, threaten their lives, hold them at gunpoint and physically assault them if they choose. Most of their charges are bogus, but systematically finagle their way through the system. Hiring and firing practices, as well as promotions, are often predicated by use of the "good ole boy system." Education and experience are excellent qualifications in most areas, but in LaGrange, having the right color skin seems to have the greatest merit.

For more than three decades, I've battled LaGrange's subtle forms of racism, not just for me, but also for my family as well. My wife received a citation for being involved in a vehicular accident in which a white man was at fault. My son, who was serving honorably in the Marine Corps, was threatened and held at gunpoint for coming home late one night. My brother was stripped of his job, career and title because the town and its leaders refused to have a "nigger" serve in the capacity of police chief. And me...well, I've had quite a few stones of discrimination tossed my way as well. Luckily for me, my rocks haven't come in the form of stones, but, rather in the form of hatred. I find solace in knowing that these rocks can only hurt me if I allow them. They are fierce and they are poignant, but their greatest impact is found in the recipient's quiet acceptance. As long as I stand firm in my fight for justice, the rocks might bruise me, but they'll never be able to break me.

www.ingramcontent.com/pod-product-compliance
Lightning Source LLC
Chambersburg PA
CBHW020919140626
46545CB00015B/930